The Mindfulness of Singing

Creating a Harmonious Mind, Body, and Spirit

Denise Ritter Bernardini, Toni Crowder

StudioBos

The information in this book is not intended to be used to diagnose or treat any medical or emotional condition. The content of this book is for informational purposes only. The authors and publisher are not responsible for any conditions that require a licensed professional. The reader should regularly consult a physician in matters relating to his/her health and particularly with respect to any symptoms that may require diagnosis or medical attention. The use of this book implies the reader's acceptance of this disclaimer.

Visit mindfulnessofsinging.com for additional resources, including the podcast, newsletter, journal, and more.

Visit studiobos.com to learn more about all of the StudioBos books, audiobooks, and podcasts.

Edited by Nancy Bos and Faith Steinfort
Published by StudioBos Media
Albuquerque, NM 87106 USA
www.studiobos.com

Copyright © 2023 by Denise Bernardini and Toni Crowder
All rights reserved.
ISBN: 9798361700394

No portion of this book may be reproduced in any form without written permission from the publisher or author, except as permitted by U.S. copyright law.

Contents

In Praise of the Book	1
Introduction	5
How to Use This Book	5
How the Book Came Together	9
Chapter 1 - Set the Stage	**13**
Singers Meditation and Affirmation	13
What Is Mindfulness?	14
Chapter 2 - Plan For Success	**22**
Journaling - Why Not?	25
Creating Goals	28
Chapter 3 - Battle of the Mind	**32**
Self-Judgment: Ridding Yourself of Out-Of-Tune Voices	41
Judgment vs. Self-Critique	44
C'aint vs. Able	47
Releasing Self-Judgment	50
Trauma - Uncovering Subconscious Saboteurs	53
Addressing Anxiety	63
Mental Fatigue - When Things Don't Go as Planned	65
Facing Resistance	68
Chapter 4 - Spirit Sets the Tone	**70**
Fear or Love - Guide the Heart	72
Breathe - Inhale the Magic	78
Breathwork Toolbox	84
Alternate Nostril Breathing	85
Humming Bee Breath	94
Breathwork Toolbox Summary	97
Meditation	101
Singer's Five Love Languages	117
Embracing the Silence	124

Chapter 5 – Body as the Instrument   **130**
   Hydration – Aqua Vita   138
   Food – Don't Listen to Mary Poppins   142
   Exercise – Move That Body   152
   Sleep – Restore Your Voice   161

Chapter 6 – Take Center Stage   **168**
   Creating the Final Harmony   168
   Closing   172

About the Authors   **179**

To all of our students - past, present, and future - we dedicate this book to you. We have been fortunate to work with hundreds of lovely, diverse, and talented individuals, and we are extremely grateful for each one. Thank you for teaching us and inspiring us to write this book. We hope and pray it will enrich your lives and help you harmonize your mind, body, and spirit into a lovely song.

To our families and friends, we are tremendously grateful for your wonderful love and support. To all of our teachers, coaches and mentors, thank you for investing in us and helping us share the love of music.

In Praise of the Book

High notes of praise, from a Critically Acclaimed Classical Singer, an Emmy Award Winning Indie-Folk-Rock Artist, and a West End Musical Theater Star, speak to the diverse appeal of *The Mindfulness of Singing*. Whether you are a hobby singer or a professional singer, get ready to ignite your inspiration and fire up your voice for creating a harmonious mind, body, and spirit!

As I have lumbered along in the development of my own singing career, I have often lamented how the very most important part of being a singer is the least addressed under our current training regimen. This is, of course, the psychological aspect, for which very few universities are prepared to train their students. We currently rely on "mentors" to prepare our young singers for what is a constantly shifting landscape of excitements, disappointments, and thrills. But unlike other instruments in which the player does not reside, singing is the greatest representation of a required mind/body connection. The voice struggles to make a sound that does not first reside in the heart and mind of its maker. The trouble of this mentor system is that it puts one's sense of self and psychological health in the hands of another, as the good mentors try to prepare their students for independence during the demanding lives of their careers.

This book offers a splendid alternative; a systematic program for the singer to build a compass for their own health and well-being, which can last them throughout their career. It is both authoritative and charmingly anecdotal, and its methods apply to singers of all levels of study. It is essentially a fun read written by two women who have had their own struggles and offer not only their own advice of how they have dealt with them, but an essential guide that can help the reader develop their own program for a life-long, healthy relationship between their hearts, minds, and voices.

Ryan de Ryke, Internationally Acclaimed Operatic Lyric Baritone
haymarketopera.org/ryan-de-ryke

The *Mindfulness of Singing: Creating a Harmonious Mind, Body and Spirit* is the most thoughtful, brilliant, and knowledgeable book I have ever read on the topic of singing. It was great to read about many practical techniques and lifestyle practices, such as how much water to drink, how to breathe properly, and what to eat in order to optimize vocal precision, performance energy and overall well-being. Not to mention, I loved the chapter on meditation. Denise and Toni did an excellent job simplifying complex topics, such as meditation, and making it crystal clear how to incorporate beneficial practices into daily life.
I highly recommend this book to anyone seeking practical fun tips on how to perform at your highest level while feeling and looking great. Hats off to Denise and Toni for putting this brilliant book together. I will find myself coming back to it over and over again.

Jillian Speece, Emmy Winning Indie Folk Rock Singer-Songwriter
thebergamot.com

IN PRAISE OF THE BOOK

After a rather serendipitous meeting during the pandemic, it became apparent to me that working with Denise and Toni would be integral in forming how my Ultimate Performance Academy™ would take shape. It would become an essential guide for the creation of my business foundation.

Being a professional singer and actor in mainstream musical theatre, I am continually searching for new ways to hone my craft. Focusing on battling the difficulties that sometimes present themselves when we are in practice with our skills has become an invaluable activity. Having tools to use when we feel that negative voice, or experience moments of doubt or challenge, to working freely in our craft, is a game changer.

Breathwork and Biohacking are such essential parts of being a vocal athlete. And *The Mindfulness of Singing* is undoubtedly an essential tool for anyone's toolbox that is looking to feel more connected to their performance.

Daniel Koek, International Musical Theatre Star
danielkoek.com

THE MINDFULNESS OF SINGING

Introduction

Some self-help books evoke new thought and new inspiration. After all, Maya Angelou said, "When you know better, do better." This book is actually a playbook. We hope you will gain some wonderful new insights, but we created this book to be immersive and experiential, just like singing. No one learned how to sing by reading a book alone. So, commit now in order to actively take part in this step-by-step guide for harmonizing your mind, body, and spirit.

How to Use This Book

In *The Mindfulness of Singing,* we provide hands-on practical tips and guidelines for both amateur and professional singers. Most vocal books focus on how to create a more beautiful tone. This book helps readers create a vibrant and more fully present lifestyle, which actually enriches and strengthens the singing voice.

During this journey, we encourage you to sing for a minimum of fifteen minutes every day. Singing is a tool for mindfulness, and it will be helpful to sing frequently in order to apply the exercises.

It is far better to be focused and consistent than to spend hours engaged in mindless singing.

This journey is created through the lens of the singer's mind, body, and spirit. Examining each of these areas creates a practice of mindfulness through singing. Each chapter will guide readers to bring more awareness to different daily habits. The Mind, Body, and Spirit themes each offer a questionnaire that facilitates an open mind and heart and helps set goals and intentions. Mind, body, and spirit are intertwined, and can be interpreted to be more than one concept. However, for continuity and focus, this book will try to maintain succinct themes.

The subchapters encourage an examination of the voice in order to promote personal growth. Each subchapter will follow with a corresponding SING Method activity. The activities provide a practical application of the information presented. Here is a step-by-step guide for using the SING Method.

***S*: Set Your Intention** - If you have ever taken a yoga class, you have probably heard the instructor invite everyone at the beginning to "set an intention." This invitation draws the yogi into a space to be present and mindful. So many times, we start on a task without clearly defining what we hope to achieve. Singing requires attentiveness to clearly articulated goals: Why do you want to sing? What do you hope to gain by singing? Once you have decided to sing, what do you hope to achieve during a particular practice session? Many students will practice their singing with no clear expectation of what they hope to accomplish at the end of each practice. Simply singing through music doesn't make a better singer. Like so many aspects of life, without clearly defined goals, we can drift along and then wonder why we haven't arrived at our desired destination. Setting intentions for singing may spill over into everyday life, yielding great benefits. Slowing down to determine intention is part of the art of mindfulness. Once this is accomplished, mindful practice while singing is more readily attainable.

I: **Isolate From Distractions** - We are living in an age where we have hundreds of distractions. The ever-present ding of the phone pulls us from the task at hand. Isolating ourselves to focus on singing is a gift we can give ourselves. Shut off the phone, the computer, the television, and any other distractions. The only thing that should make sound is you.

Clearing away the external distractions is the easy part. The actual work begins when we shut down all the internal distractions, the choir of voices inside our head telling us what we can and can't do. There are many paths to quieting the choir. For authentic practice and joy during singing, silence the distractions. The degree to which we can quiet those voices is a great indicator of how mindful we are in the present moment. This takes practice. If you are new to mindfulness, don't allow frustration with this new mindset to keep you from moving forward.

N: **Notice Your Body** - Be present in your body. Where are the tensions? Is there resistance? From where does it arise? How are these attached to the physicality of singing? Is the resistance the mind's reluctance to give up control? This need to control what is happening with sound is an illusion. To have a beautiful sound, stop trying to control the outcome. The opposite of control is freedom. Let go! Put intention and breath behind each sound and shut out the ego and its need to keep you in a compliant box. Don't let the ego dictate the process.

G: **Give Up Judgment** - The *Singers Meditation and Affirmation* states: "in this moment I give up judgment." What if practice time became a judgment-free zone? What if we could step back from ourselves and see our mistakes as areas for future growth? Judging is placing a good or bad, right or wrong label on everything. Practicing mindfulness and being genuinely aware can take away the shame or fear accompanied by judgment. Once you have completed the SING Method there is space for mindfulness and personal growth. Remember too, this is time to have fun! Arriving at practice time with an attitude of "Now I must try hard to create the right sound" takes away mindfulness. Let go of the need for perfection and embrace the joy of singing.

Following each SING Method section, there are questions as a journaling guide. If the questions lead you down a completely different path, take it. You never know what you may find along the journey.

Perhaps in the past, you considered singing simply as a fun activity to enjoy with friends or as a commitment to worship or a community choir. Maybe you studied singing as a career path. Whatever the case, step in and surrender past ideas of why or how to sing and open yourself up to a holistic mindfulness practice that also helps you develop a love of singing.

We are grateful to welcome you to our community. We hope you use our book to sing your face off and create an enriched lifestyle through *The Mindfulness of Singing*.

The components of our SING Method are found within the simple meditation in Chapter One. We have set the prayer to music, which is available on the website. We encourage you to log on and sing along to set your intention of gratitude, joy, wonder, and play before singing. To hear the meditation, go to the mindfulnessofsinging.com.

How the Book Came Together

From Denise:

In 2017, I was in chronic pain and could barely walk. I had been diagnosed with stenosis of the spine and the orthopedic surgeon wanted to fuse four of my vertebrae. This was unacceptable to me. I told him I wanted physical therapy for six weeks first. If I wasn't better after that, I would be back to discuss the surgery. You must understand there wasn't a day that didn't go by without me literally crying in pain. My right leg and foot had stopped working and were constantly in debilitating nerve pain. It highly motivated me to find a new path to wellness.

Prior to this, I had been very active and walked three or four miles every day. I didn't realize that I needed to change my diet, as it was causing inflammation in my body, and I needed to deal with my stress in a more constructive way. As a response, I began reading a lot of books about food as medicine, and I meditated again. That is when I discovered breathwork.

Toni, my long-time friend, had been in Italy off and on over the last few years and while we stayed in contact, she was unaware of my back issue. Fast forward, she is home in the States, and we wanted to see each other. Low and behold, we were both geeking out about breathwork and nutrition and how they affected one's singing. Therefore, it seemed natural to me to twist her arm and force her to write this book with me. At least that's how I see it. I'll let her tell her version of the events.

From Toni:

Denise and I met in graduate school in Texas, but we forged the real depth of our friendship as roommates at a summer opera training program. If you know anything about summer programs, you understand the old adage applies — people bond during times of adversity. Since graduation, we had lived nowhere near each other and only kept in touch occasionally. One day, Denise called to share with me she was moving to Virginia. This was just about the same time that I was selling my home in Virginia. As fate would have it, we both were in the same state for just a couple of months.

One day we were visiting, and she said to me, "I have an idea." This didn't surprise me, as one of Denise's many gifts is that she is a perpetual creator. Denise always has an idea brewing. She said, "I think we need to write a book about the mindfulness of singing." I thought, hmm... not a bad idea. With a little encouragement from Denise, I was on board; but I didn't realize then what a significant impact that little suggestion would have on my life. I had already discovered over the years that the singing journey was about so much more than the actual physical process of singing. For me, personally, singing is a tool that guides me in bringing more awareness to my mind, body, and spirit.

I assumed we would knock the book out quickly, and then I would be on my merry way back to Italy. But that was the spring of 2020, so of course, COVID-19 derailed my plans. Before COVID, I envisioned meeting people from around the globe during my nomadic adventures. After COVID, thanks to Denise's idea, we did actually get to meet people from around the globe, virtually, through the *Mindfulness of Singing* podcast. Our book, podcast, website, and playshops provided me with a wonderful diversion from my original journey. I am grateful for this journey and I hope that your adventure into the Mindfulness of Singing will yield many rewards.

Chapter One

Set the Stage

Singers Meditation and Affirmation

Thank you for this moment.
I set my intention to be completely present right here now.

I am incredibly grateful for this moment
To rest in the presence and play in the sound of my unique voice.

I seek only to express myself
In the most authentic way.

Staying centered, awake, alert, and attentive,
I listen to my spirit and my own inner wisdom.

I choose only to express myself
Through love, care, and compassion.

I release all judgment of myself
And those who seek to guide me.

And I let go of perfection to embrace this sacred practice
Of being fully present with my voice.

What Is Mindfulness?

Mindfulness is not one thing: this or that. Instead, it is noticing, being present, and aware in the moment. Even better, it is about being present in many moments. It is, perhaps, most often used as a path to personal transformation. Singing is an act of mindfulness that may compel and draw us forward, bringing awareness to every area of life. Mind, body, and spirit are all brought more fully into consciousness through the practice and art of singing. Singing is, possibly, one of the ultimate tools for practicing mindfulness.

With the study of any other instrument, it is easy to detach oneself. However, the voice is a piece of our quintessential being. Like the snowflake, it possesses its own beauty and individuality. With the piano, flute, guitar, etc., a musician can blame something else for the success or failure of the instrument. There is nothing more vulnerable, fragile, or delicate than analyzing the completely separate, individual "thumbprint" of our voice. Thus, mindfulness gives us a useful tool to look inward at our own voice's individuality and to practice cultivating a better relationship with ourselves through singing.

Since the voice is an integration of mind, body, and spirit, it brings a need for an individualized practice of mindfulness. Just as no two people have the same voice, no two people have the same method of mindfulness. One cannot have a beautiful, moving voice without doing the work mentally, physically, and spiritually. Mindfulness can help. Through mindfulness, the journey of singing can bring rich rewards far outside of the actual technical aspects of singing.

Imagine yourself as a high-wire performer. You would notice each movement of the foot and toe. The ankle and legs would need to work a certain way, and the hips and body would have to be in perfect alignment. You could not afford for your mind to wander. It could cause you to fall and plummet to your death! One lapse in attention could cost you your life. What better incentive to be mindful—death or paying attention? This visualization shows how mindfulness or awareness is accomplished... if your life depends on it. For most of us, our life doesn't rely on it, but sometimes our peace of mind certainly does.

Even though you might not be a high-wire performer, you have probably had similar experiences. For instance, maybe you paint or play golf. Painters use brushes as an extension of themselves and their creative energy and vision. Golfers multi-task, thinking about posture, hand position, and how the feet are grounded. Both examples use the body as an extension of their intention and creativity. Often the key is to not overthink but to rely on instinct and sensations. The more relaxed and mentally present, the greater the likelihood that you will connect with the ball, and it will sail down the fairway. Doesn't that sound familiar?

When being mindful or practicing meditation, time seems to slow down. Senses become heightened. Just think about when you try to meditate. You suddenly notice every itch and minor discomfort — your mind shifts. The ego tries to take you back to the chatter and wants to tether you to your usual state of "monkey brain." If you practice mindfulness, you find that improvement comes over time. Baby steps are the way here. Don't expect significant changes all at once.

The truth is, we have all been in the mindful zone even if it was just momentary. This state is called flow. The world seems to fade away. Often after this experience, we want to do it again as soon as possible. All too often, life and business get in the way. Singing can get you there again!

Artists, athletes, and singers get into what many call "flow state." Can you recall a moment when you've been entirely wrapped up and time flew? Did you forget yourself, and the thing you were doing became effortless? Athletes call this the "zone." You don't need to become a golfer, tightrope artist or painter to be mindful. You only need to decide you want to pursue the practice of mindfulness.

By choosing to sing as a new way to experience awareness, you will find ways to connect with your inner calm and be mindful, too. The great thing is, you don't have to be a singer by trade or hobby. You can be a person whose talents lie elsewhere. You can choose to sing and see where it takes you on your journey.

In Mihaly Csikszentmihalyi's book *Flow: The Psychology of Optimal Experience* he says, "The best moments in our lives are not the passive, receptive, relaxing times… The best moments usually occur if a person's body or mind is stretched to its limits in a voluntary effort to accomplish something difficult and worthwhile."

According to *Medical News Today*, "Flow has similarities with mindfulness, as both involve a focus on the present moment. However, people often use the term "flow" in reference to situations in which they are being productive, whereas a person can be in a state of mindfulness regardless of whether or not they are doing a task."

Csikszentmihalyi is often considered the "father of flow." In the 1970s he examined people who did activities solely for pleasure. His studies developed into the following flowchart.

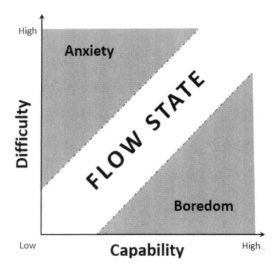

While the primary focus of this book is mindfulness, we couldn't leave out flow. Perhaps your singing in the past was filled with difficult experiences, or perhaps you sang professionally and along the way you got in a rut by not adding novelty. We hope you will find the sweet spot that marries mindfulness and singing, and ride the wave of experiencing flow.

Mindfulness is allowing ourselves the opportunity to slow down, step outside ourselves, and observe what we are doing. We all know the saying, "Practice makes perfect." Here's a little secret you may have already discovered for yourself: That statement isn't true.

Simply practicing anything, whether it's breathwork, singing, yoga, or fly-fishing, doesn't actually make you perfect. As Einstein said, "Insanity is doing the same thing over and over and expecting different results" and unfortunately a great deal of "practicing" is simply repetition that may or may not be serving you.

We want to encourage you to get in the sandbox and play! Throw out all the rules of practicing anything and pay more attention to your own body's feedback. Unfortunately, some of us think we must "practice" in an exact set way. Take a fresh look at the way you practice and make sure your habits are serving you.

Perhaps your practice session looks like:

- (✓) 20 minute warm up
- (✓) Sing the hardest song first
- (✓) Aggressively mark all mistakes and beat yourself up about it

Try instead starting with a guided meditation, or a stretch, get relaxed and give yourself permission to just be present and have fun. Then write all the things you did well, and even jot down all the things you loved about your voice.

Challenge/Skills Ratio

Our ability to focus and be most engaged is when the difficulty of the task and our skill set are at a very specific relationship. Many times, people give up on studying something because they feel it is too difficult and are overwhelmed. On the flip side, if the task is too easy, we can stop concentrating. The midpoint of these opposites is flow. When we are in flow, we are in a magical place where the task causes us to stretch, but not to snap.

To dare is to risk losing one's footing momentarily.
Not to dare is to lose oneself.

Soren Kierkegaard

Denise thought I (Toni) had absolutely lost my mind when I called to share about my latest upcoming grand adventure. With loads of excitement, I told her I was going to attend the Flow Genome Project's Flow Canyon program. This meant I would hike the San Rafael Swell in Utah for a week-long training with the wild outdoors as our classroom. I would only have the clothes on my back and a 35-pound backpack loaded with camping equipment. Camping equipment does not mean mascara, lipstick, deodorant, or toilet paper! At this point, Denise said, "Well good for you; you go ahead and have a great time! I'll be home enjoying my indoor plumbing and daily showers. Let me know when or if you make it up out of that canyon!"

I was honored to travel the desert canyon with a small, but mighty, amazing tribe of individuals, all committed to studying leadership and flow states. It truly was an incredible once-in-a-lifetime experience, and it ticked all the boxes for triggering flow:

1) Complete Concentration in the Moment - The last day of the hike was very intense. Every step mattered for my safety, and the safety of others. Looking back at how far we traveled up from the bottom of the canyon was immensely cathartic. I thought, if I can physically do that, what emotional canyons can I climb out of as well?

2) Immediate Feedback - The weather gave us immediate feedback every step of the way. While we hiked in June, we still experienced snow and rain. Remember, we only had the clothes on our backs, so planning was crucial. We also had to pay very close attention to the environment as there were no road signs or GPS. We only had our topographical map.

3) Clear Goals - I had one clear goal - survival. I maintained a heightened sense of awareness that my actions had clear and significant consequences for myself and my group. I still remember the learning curve of packing that beastly backpack. It was an art form. My care of the camping supplies mattered for me and my team.

4) The Challenge-Skills Ratio - As the Csikszentmihalyi chart stated, this experience placed me directly in the flow zone, as I had very little hiking experience - certainly nothing as demanding as hiking out of a canyon! However, I had already attended Flow Genome Camp and had met the leaders who were extreme outdoor aficionados, including a former Navy Seal. This eased my anxiety because I knew I was in good hands. It was the perfect balance of stretching me completely out of my comfort zone without making me feel so overwhelmed or fearful that it discouraged me. In fact, one of my teammates said at the end, "Courage isn't the absence of fear, it's feeling the fear, and doing it anyway. And Toni, I could certainly see you taking every step today despite your fears."

Many people might say they would love to experience a deep flow state. The reality, however, is getting into a deep flow state requires getting out of our comfort zone; and many don't want to leave the nest of comfort or habit to embrace the possibility of flow. Uncertainty is our rocket fuel, but it doesn't have to be as dramatic as a canyon adventure.

Jaime Wheal, founder of the Flow Genome Project and author of *Recapture the Rapture: Rethinking God, Sex, and Death in a World That's Lost Its Mind* states that "to unlock boredom, seek novelty, make art and be of service." All three tasks can be obtained through singing.

Chapter Two

Plan For Success

In this chapter we will guide you to be in the best position for implementing the information found in this book. We will help you set the stage to complete the objectives laid out in each chapter.

We know that taking on new challenges and changes can be tricky and might even cause anxiety. However, if you set your mind to seeing what this book has to offer as a fun and exciting adventure, we think you will be less prone to feel nervous about what this book may elicit. We want to help you prepare for the best success by giving you a plan of action. Practicing mindfulness is often thought of as "10 minutes of breathing or meditation," but it can permeate your entire life. You may ask: How does this pertain to singing? When you put mindfulness into every part of your life, change becomes inevitable and without a lot of effort, because you are being aware. All of which deeply impact us as singers. The voice is so much more than moving sound through the larynx; it is who we are, our essence, our very being. This awareness will make you a better singer because you will be more in tune with your mind, body and spirit. Let's walk through the prep work of why, when, where, what, and how. Taking the time to plan for success will be extremely important in your transformational journey.

Why - You must be sure "why" you have taken on this challenge. As we mentioned earlier, there are many reasons to sing, but for our purposes, the "why" is to improve mindfulness. You might be pleasantly surprised with what happens to your voice when you improve your ability to be mindful.

When - You may find that there's an optimal time for you to sing. Everyone has a Biological Peak Time or BPT. Denise's BPT is in the evening. For Toni, it is in the morning. Most people do not do well in the afternoons during that 2:00–4:00 slump. Give yourself the best opportunity to be successful by assessing what time would be best for you.

Where - It's important to prepare your space for minimal distractions and maximum peace. Many people want to be in a private space when they practice. If you are constantly distracted by worrying about who is listening to you, or someone else's activity interrupts you, perhaps a change of time or environment might be more productive. To ensure your success, be certain your BPT and your surroundings will work well together. Once you have chosen your space, here are some specifics for getting the room ready.

Declutter - Remove unnecessary items out of the room that may distract you or make you feel anxious. Think of Marie Kondo, what can you part with that isn't serving you anymore? The act of decluttering the workspace and having it ready to go helps keep the intention that you have set for yourself. Many people believe that a disorganized and cluttered space distracts the mind and drains energy. If you clear the "clutter" (papers, files, other documents) off your desk, then you can focus and won't be reminded of other tasks.

Lighting - Have multiple sources of light so that you can choose bright light for music or low light for improvisation. Candlelight might be your choice for a peaceful experience.

Color - Choose to surround yourself with calming colors. Personalize your space by putting things you love around you. There is something powerful about having an area that is yours and declaring it a stress-free zone.

What - What, specifically, would you like to sing? Singing something because you "should" or because everybody loves that song, but you really hate the piece is counterproductive. Pick some songs that really speak to you and suit you well. Perhaps there is a song you have always wanted to sing but haven't. Now is the time! Go for it. This is about you, your growth and your pleasure, so please have fun!

How - Unfortunately the word "practice" sometimes has a very negative connotation for many people. We can all probably remember some activity we were forced to do as a child and practicing was certainly no fun. Maybe for you, it was the dreaded piano lessons. Perhaps you had to sit at the piano for an entire thirty minutes until the kitchen timer rang. Or maybe it was hours of practice on the sports field doing endless drills when you were hot and tired. We hope you will rethink any negative connotations you have about the word "practice" and replace them with the word "play."

We want to encourage you to improvise and try new things. Please throw every negative thought about practice out the window and replace it with the fresh air of creativity and pleasure. Forget all the rules. Listen to your own body. Become a scientist in the laboratory of discovering your own sensations when you sing. We can't stress enough that how you practice or play is truly the essence of mindfulness. Let the playtime begin!

A famous line in a song from the 1970s singer Karen Carpenter sums it up very well:

> Don't worry that it's not
> Good enough for anyone else to hear
> Just sing, sing a song

Speaking of a playful spirit, journaling can be fun and not scary or overwhelming. You might even find yourself smiling while you write.

Journaling – Why Not?

We both will admit that journaling is not something we have readily embraced. Toni used journaling as part of a group studying *The Artist's Way* by Julia Cameron. You might consider her book in addition to *The Mindfulness of Singing* for your ongoing journey. Denise was at a women's retreat a few years ago, and one speaker talked about journaling. Denise quit listening as soon as the presenter mentioned the word journaling, and Denise would agree that she can be rude like that sometimes.

We have always associated journaling with the same mentality as the teenage diary. Who cares? Silly little girl dreams that aren't realistic. We also have connected it with narcissism. Our thoughts have always been that no one is going to give two hoots about our journal. Nor do they care about our opinions, feelings, or aspirations. We are pretty sure no one is going to find our journals in 100 years and say WOW! What a memoir! After all, we know what we want, and we don't need to write it down. In many ways, this is closed-minded to what the purpose of journaling serves and the spirit in which it is intended.

Denise recently found a journal in a box of "junk," and it was written in 1993. A long, long, long time ago. Imagine how surprised she was when she opened the journal and found a list of goals and dreams. Guess how many of those were accomplished? We are not saying something "magical" happens when you write it down, but damn, that was some "MAGIC." Denise achieved every one of those written goals, even a couple that had been forgotten. We know that sounds weird, but there is something on a spiritual level and certainly on a subconscious level when you put pen to paper.

What we object to is the daily recording of minutiae, like "today I bought asparagus and went to the park" or "I hate my spouse, who is incapable of picking up socks." These kinds of documentation are really just whining, in our humble opinions, and are not about the HARD inner-work that we all need to do on OURSELVES. If your spouse doesn't pick up socks, that's not on you. Writing it down just makes it more prominent in your mind. What you want to be writing about are your goals, aspirations, and people/things for which you are grateful.

Tony Robbins states that "Setting goals is the first step in turning the invisible into the visible." A study by Dr. Gail Matthews provides empirical data to support the practice of writing goals. In this study, 76 percent of the participants who wrote their goals successfully achieved their goals. There are many popular tools for writing goals. Many of them are acronyms such as SMART, CLEAR, DUMB, etc. The important takeaways from all of these methods are that they need to be realistic, simple, motivating, attainable, and timely. What matters too, is that you are honest with yourself and trust your own instincts.

We encourage you to create some goals, but we also encourage you to ask yourself, "Why is this important to me?" Your goals should serve the best version of yourself. The human condition can make us aspire to things that bring us love, admirers, recognition, or make us feel worthy. If you don't love and admire yourself, then all the goal planning in the world will not make you happy. Also, remember that you stand a chance of accomplishing your goals if you are mindful of the outcome. For instance, while you might lose ten pounds in one week, it would be great to analyze whether this will really serve you in the long run. When we lose ten pounds quickly, we increase the likelihood of putting them back on. A more manageable and healthy goal of one pound per week will be an achievable long-term goal.

Creating Goals

Use the SING Method to find out what your goals really are:

S: **Set Your Intention** - Ask yourself: "What is the goal?"

I: **Isolate From Distractions** - Spend some quality time sitting with this query.

N: **Notice Your Body** - Does the goal make you feel big and expansive or small and afraid?

G: **Give Up Judgment** - Don't let your inner critic say you can't do this or that. If you can dream it, it feels right and good for you, then write it down!

Grant Cardone, best-selling author of *The 10X Rule: The Only Difference Between Success and Failure*, has a special trick: he writes his goals down twice a day — once in the morning, and then once again at night. He explains, "I want to wake up to it. I want to go to sleep and I want to dream with it... I want to write my goals down before I go to sleep at night because they are important to me, they are valuable to me and I get to wake up to them again tomorrow."

Another popular method for getting clear on your goals is to create a vision board. You know the saying "a picture is worth a thousand words." We don't believe that simply cutting out a picture of what you want will make it happen. However, what would happen if you combined a vision board exercise with clearly written SMART goals, and put action behind your vision? Data suggests you would be very successful at achieving your goals. Here is a review or perhaps an introduction to the acronym SMART:

S - Specific

M - Measurable

A - Achievable

R - Realistic

T - Time sensitive

Sometimes people have to take things to the extreme to get really clear on their dreams. I created a bobblehead Toni book in 2010. I made multiple copies of a picture of just my head and yes, you guessed it, glued them to the images of the things I wanted to see happen in my life. Then I wrote about them. Later I came back and added the dates for when all the events occurred. I am a minimalist, and I have thrown away most of the things from my past; but this book is priceless to me. As the acronym states: get specific on what you want, make sure you can measure it so that you know when it happens, be clear that it is achievable, relevant, and that there is a specific time frame for your goal.

You might think that we have both achieved all of our goals. Nope. Not even close. We are both overachievers and competitive, so we are always trying to do something new, bigger, and better. But, guess which goals are still not in our grasp? Yep, the ones we didn't write or weren't clearly detailed. Of course, you bet we have now. In fact, we are still writing things down because we are still not perfect and still have things we want to achieve. Before you say we are nuts, understand that we know that to achieve goals, we have to put action into the mix. The magic of journaling doesn't happen without a particular recipe for success. The recipe goes something like the one that follows.

MAKING YOUR GOALS

Ingredients

- 1 CUP GOAL SETTING
- 1 CUP JOURNALING
- 1 CUP STRATEGY
- ½ CUP NETWORKING

This may be oversimplified, but without writing things down it will be difficult to know how much you have progressed. If you are still not convinced, here are a few more reasons:

- When you journal, document the little gems or details that show you what you really value and desire. These details will provide you with some insight not only into who you are, but what will motivate you. You will see on paper your truth.
- The practice of writing things down, even if it is just a sentence or two, will help you declutter your mind. You will become clearer and more focused.

- Mental health professionals say that when they let their clients just talk, they often talk themselves into the solution to their problem. Journaling can serve the same purpose. It usually gives you clarity on an issue or a way to see things from another point of view.
- Journaling allows you to track your overall development. We hope with the use of this book you will see how far you have come when you go back and read your daily entries in your journal. Sometimes it can even help you see patterns in your actions you may not want to repeat. When it comes to our faults, we usually have a pretty short memory.

Maybe to encourage your journaling practice, you could buy a killer journal and a beautiful pen. Perhaps you would like to use the *Mindfulness of Singing Companion Journal* created specifically for this book. The way a good pen feels in your hand can be inspiring. There are many beautiful, personalized options to get excited about. So onward! Happy journaling, happy singing, happy mindfulness, and happy personal growth! (Fist pumps here)! Go play!

Chapter Three

Battle of the Mind

Sometimes to understand, or to prompt introspection, it is beneficial to take personal inventory. The following quiz can help you discover where you are in your quest for control over your mind, thoughts, and values. If you take the exact same quiz again tomorrow you might get a very different score as your emotions can make you feel differently every day. In fact, the ability to control our mind starts by observing our thoughts and emotions. It is a battle we will fight our entire lives.

Before you take the quiz, take a deep breath and then set an intention to be completely honest with yourself. Remember, you don't have to share your results with anyone, and the more honest you are the better chance you will have in discovering areas for growth and exploration. The goal isn't a perfect score, but instead a score that shows you a clear mirror for reflection.

Circle the most appropriate response and assign points as indicated:

2 points - Agree
1 point - Agree Sometimes
0 points - Disagree

I am self-confident	Agree	Agree Sometimes	Disagree
I am rarely judgmental of myself	Agree	Agree Sometimes	Disagree
I am happy most days	Agree	Agree Sometimes	Disagree
I take full responsibility for my life	Agree	Agree Sometimes	Disagree
I have addressed the traumatic events in my life	Agree	Agree Sometimes	Disagree
I am courageous	Agree	Agree Sometimes	Disagree
I am mentally tough	Agree	Agree Sometimes	Disagree
I hold myself accountable	Agree	Agree Sometimes	Disagree
I am aware of my good points	Agree	Agree Sometimes	Disagree
I am flexible and can alter my plans when things don't go my way	Agree	Agree Sometimes	Disagree

Now that you have taken the quiz, what was your score?

    20 – 14   This is a pretty strong score! Keep going.

    13 – 7   There are some areas that need to be addressed.

    6 – 1   You are really hurting, and we suggest you seek some professional help.

How do you feel about your score? Does your personal view of your mental well-being match your score? There is no right or wrong answer. If there were specific issues that jumped out at you, keep those in mind and see what suggestions may serve you best.

Thoughts become things.

Bob Proctor

Since the war for your mind will continue to surface as long as you are a human, we wanted to give you some weapons for the battle. Here are ABCs to consider for practicing controlling your mind and thoughts:

- Analyze Your Thoughts
- Block Self-Limiting Beliefs
- Change Your Focus

A: Analyze Your Thoughts - You Are in Control

Understand that you are in control of your state of being. What? We know you think the guy you work with causes you to feel a certain way, or your siblings or parents trigger negative reactions. However, there are techniques you can use to bring better awareness to your thinking, which influences not only your thoughts but also the somatic sensations you are experiencing.

Therapists and psychologists use this technique all the time. It is called CBT or cognitive behavior therapy. CBT works to teach people new behaviors by bringing awareness to their less than optimal actions and reactions. In order to be successful at this concept we must know the influences and factors that cause us to do things that are not in our best interest. Embracing self-awareness, even if it is painful, can drive lasting and productive happiness. Perhaps you have been putting off practicing because you don't "feel" like it. When you realize you are in control of your thoughts, you may be able to dive deeper and discover the reason you don't "feel like practicing."

Notice your thoughts and emotions - how do they connect to your behavior? It is easier to ignore negative emotions in an effort to control your thoughts or somatic sensations, but this will actually create more problems in the long run. When you feel something big - negative or otherwise - ask yourself: What is this emotion? If you are anxious, sad, angry, feel it. Learn from it. Other questions to ask yourself are: Does this feel familiar? Where did I learn this emotion? Sometimes recognizing the root cause can help us pinpoint what is really going on in the moment. Resist the urge to be nonchalant about the negative experience or feelings. Embrace the present emotion no matter how painful it may be.

Maybe you are already more enlightened than we are, and you don't have too many negative thoughts, (call us - we want to know how you do it). But even the enlightened can wake up on the wrong side of the bed occasionally. Seriously, we have all experienced a grumpy morning. When this happens, you may wonder why you can't seem to get out of the bad mood. It may be difficult to pinpoint any direct cause. Was it a lack of sleep, something you dreamed or ate? In any case, people will not appreciate your presence if you keep up the bad mood. What to do? Sing!

Have you ever heard of "priming the pump?" There is a law of physics that comes into play every time you make a cup of coffee in a K-cup dispenser or when you get water out of a well. Pump priming is either a manual or automatic process by which air in a pump is removed by filling it with liquid. The liquid fills the pump so that the air, gas, or vapor are removed. This is how the term originated.

Remember, the body, mind and spirit are all interwoven. Priming engages the mind by first engaging the body. You can do this by taking several deep, cleansing breaths to cultivate a positive physical state; or you could sing and hum to warm-up not only the voice, but also the mood cultivator - the mind. As you focus on your breath, voice, and physical state you are better equipped to clear your mind and focus your thoughts on the present moment. As you practice this consistently, you find that it becomes intuitive. You have literally put in positive feelings, leaving no room for negativity. The pump has been primed.

B: Block Self-limiting Beliefs - You Are the Church

As you build mindfulness practices into your day-to-day life, you may discover some of the self-limiting beliefs that have impeded your personal growth and outlook on life. Beliefs are complicated and often stem from our nature, nurture, cultural influences, and traumas both big and small. Beliefs can be powerful in shaping how we view ourselves, the world, and how we fit into it. We form beliefs about what we can and can't accomplish. It is part of human nature to accept our beliefs without questioning them. After all, we are brainwashed from birth to accept certain limitations.

Mindfulness practices help us address this tendency to see ourselves as "less than." Instead of accepting preconceived notions, commit yourself to investigating the validity of what you hold to be true to determine whether those beliefs are the product of something that does not accurately reflect who you are or want to be.

C: Change Your Focus - You are the Creator

We are not saying that your thoughts and emotions will always be positive. Life is hard; sometimes your situation sucks. It would be silly to tell you to ignore the difficult things around you. There is a new school of thought in psychology: positive thinking can be toxic and non-productive. The proponents of this school believe that if one is ignoring the things that need to be addressed by "thinking positive" the outcome can be disastrous. However, if you can focus on what is good around you and address the negative, you can reduce your stress and perhaps even that low-lying feeling of depression.

For example, there was a couple in a small village who had a house on a tiny hill. It was a modest home with only two rooms, but being on that small hill gave them a nice view of the village below. In the evenings they would open the doors and sit on their little front step and enjoy a beverage after a long day. One summer an unusual monsoon poured down on the village sweeping away many of the villager's homes. Some lost everything; others had major water damage. The couple on the hill however got lucky. The only things they lost were their steps and, from their perspective, the view of some of the hill. The storm caused them to lose their view of the village. This made them both sad. How could they sit outside now and enjoy their afternoon tea and their superior view? What could they do? They couldn't afford new steps and they especially couldn't afford to raise the house up on stilts or have it moved to the top of the hill. The couple moped and grumbled for several days. They didn't go into the village or work. They didn't want the villagers to know they lost their view. After all, it was better than everyone else's.

One day a villager came up to see if they were alright. The villager was smiling, he embraced them and laughed and said "I am so happy that you are alive and well!" The couple frowned and said, "Oh we are fine but our house lost its steps and our superior view. We are so sad and angry at the gods for taking our view from us. We must have terrible luck, and everyone will know that we have somehow angered the gods." The villager's face changed from happy to disappointed. The couple saw the look on his face and the woman said with a sarcastic tone, "You must have done ok, your home must be fine. Why else are you so content?" The villager looked puzzled and said "You must not know about what happened in the village. The hill you love was swept away and the dirt and mud came into the village and filled almost everyone's homes. Everything is lost, what the mud didn't destroy, the water washed away. Many of the facades of the homes are standing but inside, the homes are unlivable. Most people lost loved ones, babies, children, grandparents. My family is lucky, our home is standing no more, but we are grateful to be alive!"

The couple was speechless. The couple felt ashamed and terrible for being so self-centered and focused on their own lives. They were so concerned for themselves and their little existence that they forgot about the villagers. They realized at that moment that they were actually wealthy beyond measure. After all, they had each other and their home.

As the story illustrates, our circumstances aren't always positive. Of course the couple can be sad about their steps, or feel disappointed about their view, but their perspective was really screwed up. If they had left their home to check on others, they would have realized just how lucky they were. They could have focused on the good rather than the bad. Choosing to see the good over the bad and practicing being grateful every day can reduce lack, fear and anger.

Like the little couple from the village, we cannot change the negative events or experiences from our past, but we can change how we perceive them in the grand scheme of things. You can learn to control your mind by embracing personal growth, change, and your perceptions. Learning how to control your mind by challenging and questioning old long-held beliefs can help you shine the light on the highest version of yourself and your self worth. Thinking about our abundance and being grateful leaves little room for negativity.

If you are unsure of how to apply the ABCs that we outlined, try this: can you see yourself in any of these following examples?

Thought: "I can't possibly sing that phrase in one breath." = negative belief: "I just don't have enough air. Something is wrong with me."

If you don't stop to analyze this thought, you could find yourself over-breathing all the time. Thus creating an incorrect coping strategy for something that wasn't even actually a problem.

Thought: "That person really upset me this morning and now I have to go to a lesson." = negative belief: "I am not in control of my focus or feelings."

If you don't stop to analyze these thoughts, you might blame the teacher for a poor lesson when you actually weren't fully present.

Thought: "That high note really sucks." = negative belief: "I'm not a good singer."

If you continue this thought before you know it you will find yourself with two singable notes.

If you apply the ABCs what are some ways you can alter the course of these perceptions? Practicing these scenarios is like Cognitive Behavior Therapy without the $100 an hour session. It gives you a new paradigm in which to react. You don't have to do the same things over and over. Maybe you can write a thought that creates a negative belief within yourself and then create a different way to proceed. This will help you notice if your battle of the mind is working for or against you, as you play this week.

Beyond the day-to-day battle of the mind, we believe that singers additionally must deal with self judgment and trauma as they significantly impact the voice.

Be curious, not judgmental.

Ted Lasso

Self-Judgment - Ridding Yourself of Out-Of-Tune Voices

If you live long enough, you will probably discover that there are things in your life that you need to address. Maybe these things are from childhood traumas or from the sheer fact that life is complicated; but we usually get tired of chasing different outcomes from the same old behavior. The singer's mind is trying to problem-solve. You may ask yourself, "Why does that sound ugly?"

or "Why is it breathy?" Maybe your voice feels tight, so you question that sensation. Perhaps you dwell on the most destructive thought of all: "Why don't I sound like him/her?" These thoughts constrict and block your improvement both as a spiritual being and as an artist trying to grow. Judging your sound as it comes from your body can be detrimental to your growth as a singer and as a person. Sometimes students who want to please will not let the teacher finish talking while trying to give instruction. Instead, they keep singing and saying, "Oh, I know what I did wrong" or "How about this, is this better?" They don't even hear what the teacher is saying because their mind is so busy judging, self-correcting, and critiquing every minor aspect of their voice.

Students who leave the judgment to the teacher inevitably make more progress because they get out of their own way. Also, because of the natural acoustics in the room, and within our own bodies, we don't really know how we sound. The sound we singers hear in our heads, added to the sound of the room, creates an acoustical perception that no one else hears. Given this, how can singers be good judges of their voices? That is why singers benefit from a teacher in the room. They need two sets of ears: their own ears to filter the music so they can integrate their part into the song; and the teacher's ears, to tell them if something could be more resonant or that a word could be clearer. Teachers are a valuable resource and can be part of the process, but getting out of your own way is as important as having someone else in the room. After all, most of your singing will be without the teacher. They can't be around 24/7. At some point, you have to trust yourself, your process, and your instincts.

We both grew up in very conservative religious families that focused on judgment. From the time we were small children, it was ingrained in us that if we weren't good little girls, we would be judged in this world and the next. We both carry an underlying sense that we can never be good enough. This manifests itself differently for us both. Toni always feels the need to please others, and I manifest this in my f*ck you attitude. We learned to create a high level of self-judgment that hasn't served either of us well in our singing journeys. We have also seen many singers defeated before they ever open their mouths by the expectations they place upon themselves. Negativity and self-criticism will not help. Judgment often leaves no room for change. Judgments are usually made with a matter-of-fact opinion.

Think of the last time you thought "that sweater is ugly," or "I did something stupid." If you can recall this kind of instance, you can probably remember feeling absolute in that thought. You didn't think there would be growth or change in that opinion. Judgment is one way we measure ourselves and others. It is very limiting and doesn't leave space for growth. Once someone makes a judgment, they seldom roll that back. Highly critical people rarely have inner peace. They are usually busy trying to get everyone to believe what they believe. If you are on Facebook or other social media outlets, then you have seen this firsthand. People want to change other people's minds on Facebook. What a waste of time.

Judgment vs. Self-Critique

Let's discuss ways not to judge. First, you have to distinguish the difference between judgment and self-critique. These are two very different concepts. One is often an overreaction and unforgiving. The other is thinking critically with empathy as the filter. One is often unrealistic in expectations; the other dwells on fact. One often looks for the conspiracy or the unfairness in life; the other looks for the silver lining and appreciates the opportunity to flex their resilience muscles.

There is a psychological phenomenon called negativity bias. It asserts that people often feel negative words or feedback more deeply than affirmations and positive experiences. Research suggests that for every negative experience we have, we need five positive experiences to convince us we are worthy or good at what we are doing. Many scientists explain this by looking at our ancestors.

In order to live in a very hostile neolithic world, we needed to be on the lookout for what could kill us. Predators, those yummy-looking berries, stagnant water, that other tribe two forests down the trail, or that cute-looking puppy with a very large mother standing by, meant potential death or harm to our ancestors. These experiences connected the dots for us and programmed our survival brain to notice and pay attention to potential downfalls. However, now that we live past 14, we could stand to shut that part of our brain down a little. As with most things, awareness is key.

What is judgment? A black or white opinion, either good or bad, with no in-between. Students often describe performances or recitals as being "terrible" because they forgot the words of verse two of one song or two phrases in a recital of 18 songs. Really? They can't enjoy the overarching accomplishment of a recital or the culmination of an entire year's work because of two phrases? If all one can think about during a performance is the moment that has passed and one is busy listening to the voice in their head saying, "you're a screw-up," the situation is probably only going to get worse. How can they be present for the rest of the song, recital, or lesson? Of course, that is not to say one can't have an opinion.

An opinion differs from judgment; it's similar to perception. Opinions are often fluid, and they can shift over time. When a belief is thought to be the truth and one expects everyone else to have that belief, it becomes an immovable judgment. This is called dogma. During the time of singing and practicing mindfulness, be aware of saying things such as, "that was awful," or "I can't sing." These are judgments that will only limit your progress. Your opinion about your voice is your perception. The listener may have an altogether different perception. Give yourself room to accept that your thoughts are being filtered through your beliefs about yourself and others that can be counterproductive at best and devastating at worst. When you can accept that everyone has a hurt that they are trying to mend, including yourself, space for compassion, empathy, and love can fill your heart. Even for yourself.

Remember, judging yourself and others will separate you from your mindfulness goals. Shaming will, too. We have all been shamed and have done our share of shaming. It is easy to shame a child. They rarely know how to fight back. I bet we all have stories we could tell. Often shaming and trauma are experienced in the same way. They are interwoven, but the shaming we have experienced can be harder to heal. Often our closest family and companions are the very ones that have shamed us. Shame sticks to us and we often give it permission to hang around. In some ways we are the authors of our own shame. When we carry our shame, and we believe those words, we can create a reality around that experience. Shame is also painful for others, especially when we carry those wounds into our relationships.

Most of us have been taught to judge and have had a lot of practice. Because of those experiences, we may believe that judgment is an acceptable practice. We see it in social and mainstream media, religious organizations, schools, the list could go on and one. We are literally programmed to be critical and judging. That's why it's easy to judge others. Our judgmental voice has been our companion most of our lives.

However, when someone else judges us, we may think, "How dare they judge me? They don't know me." A person might feel attacked or, perhaps you are a rare person and don't care what others think. Most of us however, struggle with the thought, "I wonder what people think of me?" We don't pause and consider how our judgment may be affecting someone else. We also don't think about how the judgment we place on ourselves affects us.

Yet our own inner voice will be twice as critical or devastatingly mean and awful. Would you be your friend? Would any of us put up with a friend or family member if they spoke to us in the same way we speak inwardly to ourselves? We usually give our family and friends the benefit of the doubt, but beat ourselves up for our shortcomings or our "hideous" voice. Doesn't that sound terrible?

A voice teacher we know, during a Master Class in front of hundreds of people, said the following to a young singer: "Why are you doing this? You have zero talent. You act as if you are the greatest thing, but in reality you have no idea how to sing. Who has been telling you that you are a decent musician? Who here in this room thinks she should stop singing, raise your hand."

How does this make you feel? Doesn't it make you feel sick? Feel that pit in your stomach? This act of shaming can be what we do to ourselves every day. So cut that shit out! Psychologically, it damages you more than anything anyone else could ever do. But what does one do if that rant comes from one's own inner critic?

C'aint vs. Able

Once upon a time, there was a little "Able," and he dreamed of singing pop music. He loved the idea of holding a microphone and singing to an audience of pop music lovers. Able had his outfit planned, too! He was going to wear this beautiful pair of red leather pants and a T-shirt that said "Long Live Rock-N-Roll" with a British flag in the background. His greatest hope was to bring love and light to his audience by singing his favorite top British boy band tunes. He visualized himself on the stage strutting around like Mick, swinging the microphone like Roger, and shaking his hair like Paul.

One day Able was planning, rehearsing, and preparing for his fabulous show. He sat at the dinner table and began to eat the lovely meal he cooked for himself. Just as he picked up his pen and pad, "C'aint" walked through the door. C'aint, who was the cooler, more sophisticated brother, asked, "Whatcha doin' bro?" Able, knowing that C'aint was always raining on his parade, shyly responded, "Oh, uh, I'm planning my concert." Able pushed the plate of food over to him, he knew that C'aint would take it anyway. Rather than fight for his meal, it was just easier to give in to C'aint.

C'aint, with a twinkle in his eye sloppily eating Able's Pasta PrimaVera, sensed Able's unsteadiness, and says, "What concert?" and then chuckles, implying, "you're such a dummy." Able, already feeling insecure, shrugs and says, "Oh, just a little concert for my friends and some people who like my voice; it's really no big deal." C'aint knowing he has already won the battle, cracks up and goes for the jugular: "That's hilarious. You know you don't sing very well. Those friends just don't know how to say no to your hair-brained ideas! You know, when you leave the room they talk about you. The truth is, they laugh about your singing. Besides, pop music is for losers, Opera is the only real way to sing! Come on man, get hip with the times!" C'aint, full and strong on the meal he just devoured, gets up from the table, leaves the kitchen, and throws the food he didn't finish to the pigs, laughing all the while. Able, starving, sad, frustrated, and now scared, mutters, "He's right. I am going to cancel the concert and stop singing. I'm really not very good."

For those of you who know this story, you know that this is an allegory. The moral of the story is don't let C'aint kill your Able! Every time you keep C'aint out of your brain, he gets weaker, smaller, and eventually silent! While Able, on the other hand, gets fed, stronger, and more capable.

In Cognitive Behavior Therapy (CBT), one of the therapeutic interventions used is the "name it to tame it" technique. This technique helps people see how their emotions and egos get in their way. There is a lot of research that backs up this robust process. What if, when you have negative thoughts about yourself, your goals, your intelligence, your voice and all the other aspects about yourself you may disparage, you name that voice "C'aint." Then name that fantastic, lovely, brilliant voice in your spirit that is the source of all inspiration "Able."

Sing Method

Releasing Self-Judgment

S: **Set Your Intention** - Your quest is to sing in a judgment-free zone. That means giving yourself a goal that you know you can achieve. Is singing new to you? If so, perhaps the goal is to simply sing. Maybe it is to memorize one song, or perhaps it is to sing without thinking or judging, and just enjoy yourself.

I: **Isolate From Distractions** - Begin each practice session this week by focusing on the affirmations of how grateful you are to be in this present moment. It is hard to be in a state of gratitude and maintain distracting negative thoughts at the same time.

N: **Notice Your Body** - When you begin to sing it may feel strange to experiment with different sounds. Perhaps you are trained classically, and new or different non-classical sounds seem silly or weird. You may even feel self-conscious. It's okay. Bring your awareness to the sensations you feel in the body or throat. Is there tension or tightness? Where do you feel tight? Remember mindfulness should be relaxing. Try to release the tension you find and think about what feels good or interesting. Focus on the good stuff.

G: **Give Up Judgment** - Begin each practice session by reading the *Singers Meditation and Affirmation*. This will help you focus your mind and prepare you to be in a place of acceptance and growth.

Thoughts are the language of the brain and feelings are the language of the body.

Dr. Joe Dispenza

Joe Dispenza makes a radical statement when he says thoughts are of the brain and feelings are of the body. That is perhaps why in voice studios we ask, "How does that feel?" Those sensations whether they are great, good, or troublesome are manifestations of freedom or tensions. Another way to say it is when we feel things in the body they are "truths" for us. Each person is unique and their experience may be different from another singer. Your experience is a fact for you, and it matters. An example might be that your jaw is rigid or that your shoulders are high and tight. These body issues may be subconscious, and you may not even be aware of the postural tension or that your jaw or mouth is rigid. This happens to everyone. It is not about how terrible you are. Tension in the body is just a sign that you need to make an adjustment. Embrace it and let go of the ego and the need to judge.

Many individuals find it quite difficult to give themselves a pat on the back. Starting your journal entry by looking for your wins will help prime the pump for discovering even more significant and small victories. After each SING Method, at least one question will be designed to discover and celebrate your success. This question will be followed by a series of repeated self-inquiry prompts. Finally, each section will conclude with a few additional questions tailored to that specific activity.

Personal Reflection

Celebrate Success: What was my biggest win in this activity? Was it finally singing again or singing for the first time in an organized fashion? If you could silence your judgmental voice to even begin this journey, that would be a victory worth celebrating!

Journal Kickstarters:
- Was I here today?
- Was I genuinely present?
- Did I judge myself throughout this time?
- Did I follow through on my intention?
- Did I get distracted by outside activity or the negative thoughts in my head?
- On the challenge/skills chart, where do I find my singing experiences?
- Where would I like to be on the challenge/skills chart?
- What do I need to do to move in the direction of my goals?

Additional Inquiry: What sections of this chapter resonated with me? What areas do I know I need to address? Perhaps it would be helpful to reread those sections to give yourself more grace for the next play session. How can you adjust your mindset for the next activity if you found yourself writing more from a place of judgment than self-critique? Onward and upward!

Trauma - Uncovering Subconscious Saboteurs

People often say, "trauma is trauma." That is true to a point. We have suffered losses on several levels. We can tell you that losing a sister or father, and watching them die at home is not the same kind of trauma as being bullied. Trauma Informed Therapy is a concept in the mental health arena. One tenant of this therapeutic modality is that everyone experiences trauma in different ways. Additionally, we are not all traumatized by the same events. You and I may experience a terrible event, and it may not traumatize me; but it may cause PTSD for you. Theorists believe it is not the event itself, but rather the thoughts and emotions that we experience.

There are many reasons why a person might stop singing for a while:

- Grief and loss
- A traumatic event, i.e. Psychosomatic mutism
- Childhood memories related to singing or making music
- Frustration
- Failure to have a major career
- Insecurities

As you can see, there are a myriad of reasons someone might abandon their singing voice. Not all are related to trauma. We will mention some of those in other chapters, but here we want to speak only of the trauma related reasons people stop singing.

Song and sound can help metabolize grief.

Barbara McAfee

Grief and Loss

Losing Denise's sister and Toni's dad made it difficult for us to sing. For two years Denise couldn't sing a note. In hindsight, we should have sung anyway. It would have been therapeutic. We may have been able to deal with our pain a little better. No one talked about how singing was therapeutic and healing at that time.

Why didn't we sing in our darkest hours? We thought in order to sing we needed to feel happy. We were wrong. More to the point, once we sang again, our trauma did not impede us in any way.

I have worked as a Board Certified Registered Music Therapist and between the two of us, Denise and I have taught music education from Kindermusik to Elderstudy programs and everything in between. Through our education and experiences we had certainly learned about the many benefits of singing to help cope with physical and emotional pain, improve lung function, enhance memory, boost immunity, create bonding in a group setting, lower stress, etc. so why on earth in the time of our deepest pain, didn't we sing for heaven's sake!?

Here's the catch. Our association with singing was generally an outward professional expression usually related to pleasure, but also high stress; and in our grief, we didn't see singing as the vibrational self-healing tool that could actually lower our stress! We also didn't feel like singing, when in actuality, singing could have been the very tool that helped us decrease our stress. The key to singing while grieving lies in when and where one sings.

The Centre for Performance Science, Royal College of Music, London, UK did a fascinating study involving 15 professional singers, which scientifically proved that low-stress and high-stress singing have contrasting effects on glucocorticoid response. Specifically, when the singers sang without an audience, they had a reduced cortisol/cortisone ratio, indicating a decrease in overall stress response.

What does this mean exactly? Cortisol is a hormone that is harmful in the body when it is constantly elevated. It is associated with fight or flight and stress. We need cortisol to run a marathon, fight a bear, or escape from a fire; but for singing? We don't think so. This is why being overly nervous is so unpleasant. We are releasing cortisol. When we sing for pleasure or for fun, cortisol is decreased. It, therefore, combats stress, makes us feel zen, and also makes us want to do the activity again.

Upon researching this subject, I discovered that Denise and I were not alone. Other singers stopped singing during dark hours of grief and loss. Danielle O'Keefe wrote a blog post for *The Psychology of It*, telling the story of her experience after her mother died when she was only 28 years old. Her journey finally led her to discover the healing benefits of singing.

"My elderly singing teacher encouraged me to continue singing through the grief, however, my heart was so heavy that I could barely speak, let alone sing; and any sound I made felt out of control. As a consequence, I barely uttered a word for the next five years."

Danielle's journey eventually led to a singing career and her research on singing and grief. She explains further: "As a singer, I was particularly interested in the way in which vocalisations could assist bereaved persons... Music reaches into a person's inner depths more easily than words (Bright 1999) and provides a safe mode to release suppressed feelings of bereavement that create tension. The act of singing and actively participating in making music requires an energy that can only come from within. This allows access to those suppressed feelings and provides an outlet for their expression. Music has been integral to the healing relief from the pain of loss, and has helped me to redefine the memories associated with my mother's death. It serves as a transitional phenomenon (Winnicott 1971) to a happy, well-adjusted life."

It doesn't matter if you are an amateur, "lover of," or a professional, you can sing for yourself! Sing to express the pain inside of you and not strictly as an artistic pursuit. If you find yourself in great pain and don't feel like singing, we hope you can take some baby steps to finding your way back home to your voice. In the breathwork chapter, we discuss humming. The process of humming creates a significant amount of nitric oxide, and it just might be the baby step to get you singing again in times of darkness.

Shame and Embarrassment

One of the other causes of a cessation of singing among musicians can be deep seated memories of shame or embarrassment. An early memory that caused Denise problems with singing was associated with the act of singing itself. Here is her story:

When I was five years old, I was supposed to sing for the church Christmas pageant. They had asked me to be Mary and walk down the aisle, holding a doll representing the baby Jesus. Once I got to the stage, I was to sit by the creche and sing "Away in a Manger." To set the scene, I will also tell you that my older sister was playing the piano. She was, and still is, one of the bright lights of my life. When I was a child, she was everything! I wanted to be her; I wanted her approval, her love, and her attention.

My obsession with her, of course, drove her crazy. I got on her last nerve. When I began to sing, I got distracted. I have no idea now what made me forget the words, but something caused me to stray mentally. As I forgot those words, I panicked. I looked at my big sis to help me as she sat at the piano, and what I saw horrified me. She was red-faced and embarrassed and looked at me like I was ruining her life. To this day this memory is as vivid as it is real. I feel anxious just relaying it to you.

Tears began to fall down my cheeks, and I threw down the poor baby Jesus as everyone in the congregation gasped. I ran out of the sanctuary and to the bathroom. I sat in the corner of that pink-tiled restroom and cried until my mother came to get me. I cried all the way home and throughout the night. I remember saying a prayer: "Dear God, I promise I will not embarrass you ever again. Forgive me for not doing my best. I will never sing again." Of course, my promise went by the wayside, just as all the other deals I made with God in moments of weakness. At some point, that childhood trauma became only a faint memory and a funny story. I only recently came to realize that this trauma has caused me a lot of problems.

I had never given that memory much thought until I heard a podcast about trauma recovery. The expert, a neuroscientist, did an exercise to help people rewire their brains and memories. While that exercise was going on, the memory came to me as if it had happened yesterday. A lightbulb came on. Could this be the reason I have terrible anxiety and stage fright just before I sing? The answer was a resounding YES! It profoundly resonated with me. That experience is why I often love preparing for a performance and a recital. But those few days and moments before the concert, I am filled with fear and dread.

I couldn't believe it! My body has been telling me I was a child about to make an embarrassing mistake; why would this affect me after all these years? I would tell myself to get over it! My mind would be right, except to "get over" something your body is doing, you must be aware and conscious of the cause. My subconscious has been telling my body that I'm in trouble and I am going to embarrass myself.

What if your subconscious is sabotaging everything you're trying to accomplish, but you haven't connected the dots and don't even know or remember why? Sometimes an event in your past can cause big or little triggers. We have seen many students and auditionees cry through an entire song. When asked, "Why are you crying?" they can't answer. They don't know. It's just a song;

you're only singing! Yet, tell that to the fight-or-flight response that is racking the body with shaking hands and knees. Or the cortisol coursing through your veins that makes your vibrato wacky and your breath ragged. Sometimes this is the body reliving a traumatic past event. The brain complies and believes the sensory information and BOOM it wracks us with anxiety and misery.

We expect bullying or abuse to bring up emotions and feelings we can't control. PTSD is real. Take the person who experienced abuse as a child. They may try to drown their pain with drugs and alcohol, not realizing that this potentially destructive behavior may stem from the faint, but ever-present, past. Maybe the trauma of being chronically bullied or beaten isn't your experience, but what if there was a teacher who shamed you and told you not to sing out, or there was a church choir director who asked you to move to the back row? Maybe it was a parent or coach who pushed you onto the stage and then withheld love and acceptance because you did not perform up to their standard. The point is: If you have unaddressed trauma, whether it is big or small, it may keep you from moving forward.

We are not licensed psychologists, but our personal experiences and the observations from our students have taught us that recovering from life-altering negative experiences is vitally important. If, after reading this chapter, you feel you have some unresolved trauma that is keeping you from singing, we encourage you to seek professional help. Know that in doing so, you are brave!

Coping Strategies

First of all let us say that stage fright and anxiety before a performance is normal. We don't know anyone who doesn't struggle with this in one way or another. The question is whether it is debilitating. The consideration should be whether your performing life suffers, when faced with an upcoming concert.

Secondly, performance anxiety can come from multiple sources. It could be an attachment to an event, an authority figure or a peer. Knowing where you are on the continuum can help. If you are uncertain, you can take a questionnaire on our website to see where you might be on the scale. People are often surprised. Remember, we need stress in our lives, there is a sweet spot to a cortisol rush. We are built to be cautious and easily frightened. After all none of us would be here if the caveman had been laid back and relaxed.

In the meantime, there are things you can do to help yourself deal with anxiety or stage fright. Often, when we are afraid or nervous, our body alignment follows. Perhaps your body shrinks and contracts as if to hide or become small. This occurs many times in juries or recitals. The subconscious is saying, "Hey, maybe no one will notice us if we shrink." More than likely, we just go to what our body knows as familiar. If you are a person with posture issues, your subconscious will tell your body to behave as if nothing is wrong. It says, "Do what we always do!" But if you have any singing experience, you know that this is not the way the singer should hold their body. An erect body with the ribcage up off the belly and the shoulders held comfortably back is the best place to start. The head should be in alignment with the ceiling. The chin should neither be tucked nor sticking out. Sometimes the subconscious screams, "Hey, I am doing this, so shut up," and the head pulls forward, or the jaw juts out.

Perhaps you are reading this book because you always wanted to sing. Maybe it is because you want to sing a solo at your spiritual community, or be better at karaoke, or you may be trying to have a professional career. In any case, if you are afraid of singing in front of others, it is helpful to do some mindful exercises that may help you cope and move forward.

Explore some activities that will help with the less than optimal conditions you experience while the body is in a state of "stage fright."

- Invite a friend over and ask them to listen to your practice. Don't ask for feedback, just be mindful of how that makes you feel.
- Let those thoughts of fear and irrational feelings go by without judging yourself.
- As in the previous chapter, slow down; what is your goal? This one takes time. When working on an intention or new thought, write it on your bathroom mirror, a whiteboard, or a post-it note, so that you see it every day.
- If you struggle with fear and anxiety and singing seems impossible, don't let yourself get caught up in unrealistic thoughts. You can get better and change your mindset. It just takes daily reflections and daily practice to get there.
- And remember, in Denise's story, baby Jesus was just a doll..

Later in the book there are more ideas for coping skills about tension and relaxation.

Inspiration

Denise has a friend who experienced Psychosomatic Mutism. This is a phenomenon that causes a person to be unable to speak despite no medical explanation. He was a professional opera singer at a major opera house and was driving when someone rear-ended him and gave him whiplash. Immediately after the crash he could not speak. Within a few days he could barely utter a sound, and could not sing. After visiting many doctors, who concluded that there was no medical reason for his mutism and that he would likely never sing again, he walked away discouraged, but determined to change the outcome.

For over two years he worked every day to speak fully and steadily, and to sing. He eventually went back to singing and began teaching voice. His story is one of determination and utter obstinance. He did not let that traumatic event steal the joy and love he had for singing.

Sing Method

Addressing Anxiety

S: **Set Your Intention** - Your goal is to create a less anxious or fearful experience when singing. Try running in place and doing some jumping jacks to help you recreate the sensation of fight or flight. Once in that heightened state, try to sing with commitment to the message you're trying to get across. As a side note, an intention can be a long-term goal. Trauma is not quickly dealt with and will not go away in a few practices.

I: **Isolate From Distractions** - If you regularly sing in front of an audience or hope to do so one day, having some strategies can help you improve. One thing that may help is learning to focus by visualizing the words of the song on the wall - seeing the words go by as you sing. Another way, perhaps for the experienced singer, can be to visualize the score measure by measure as the performance unfolds. Both are strategies to stay in the present moment.

N: **Notice Your Body** - When you sing do you feel nervous or afraid? Where are these sensations manifesting? Do you overcompensate and get rigid? Or do you shrink and melt into the ground? Where do you think these somatic sensations came from? Do you know? Can you reframe the experience? If you don't know, it's ok. Experiment with different positions like lying on the floor, or sitting in a comfy chair. The goal is to relax as you sing. Once your nerves are calm, try singing again. If you need to sing in the chair or lying on the ground - who cares? The aim is to relax and give the body a new sensation to hold on to for future singing.

G: **Give Up Judgment** - If you have sung laying down or sitting and feel defeated by this don't give in to the judgment. Getting over stage fright or singer's nerves is not an easy task. It may take some time for the brain to trust the neurological messages it is getting from the body. Be kind and gentle with yourself as you teach the brain and the body a new trick. Singing is JUST singing, not slaying a dragon.

Personal Reflection

Celebrate Success: What one tiny or big positive thing did I discover in my singing? Was I able to release any anxiety? Remember, the goal is baby steps. Simply noticing tension in your shoulders is the first step in releasing that tension. If you are singing more frequently, that's a step worth celebrating.

Journal Kickstarters:
- Was I here today?
- Was I genuinely present?
- Did I judge myself throughout this time?
- Did I follow through on my intention?
- Did I get distracted by outside activity or the negative thoughts in my head?
- How can I be more consistent with this practice?

Additional Inquiry: What can I do to continue releasing anxiety? Sometimes we are so caught up in the moment that we can't even tell where our anxiety manifests in the body. Your phone can become a fantastic teacher. Don't be afraid to record yourself! Gather up your courage and video your next play session. This might provoke anxiety and help you delve even deeper into your areas of self-judgment. Remember, you can always delete the video. This is only for your own personal growth. You can do it!

Mental Fatigue - When Things Don't Go as Planned

We wish we could tell you that once you have taken control of your judgemental inner critic and have addressed any underlying trauma issues, you would then be home free in the battle of the mind. Unfortunately, it's never that easy. Life doesn't always go as planned. We think we are so in control, but life throws us curve balls all the time. Life's daily mild disruptions and major significant changes can all have a huge impact on our mental process and on our desire to sing.

Our thoughts create our feelings, which shape our emotions, which create our actions. When the flow in that pipeline is positive, it's easy to sing. Singing isn't merely a tool to enhance the mind, body, and spirit; it is also a fantastic barometer that can continuously tell us where we are in life's overall journey. If we don't feel like singing, we can stop and analyze the resistance.

The first step is to simply be aware of what we are thinking and feeling. Is this disruption or feeling of resistance significant? Can I own what I am feeling, embrace it and then move past it to something different? Is my mental fatigue more physical (lack of sleep, hunger, etc.) or is my resistance more psychological? (fear, boredom, depression, etc.)

We have identified a "five-minute theory." This theory claims that the most difficult time in a task is the time to just get started. Those five little minutes can mean the difference between doing the activity or talking ourselves out of it. If we can push through that resistance, the reward will usually come to us. The question is, can we be determined and find wholeness? Toni ran two half marathons and always felt like the first mile was the worst. Sometimes the hardest part is simply getting your tennis shoes on and getting out the door.

As you begin to practice (or as we mentioned earlier "play") you will face times of resistance. Sometimes things will simply not go as planned and you will not feel like singing. During those times the most challenging part of practicing is getting started. Here are some questions and tips to guide you through the resistance;

1. Is my resistance physical? - Can I change my physical state? Can I eat a snack or take a power nap? Could I use a quick breathwork activity to help increase my energy or calm my anxious state? (see breathwork examples in the Spirit chapter)

2. Is my resistance emotional? - Do I need a moment to talk through what I am feeling? Am I procrastinating because I am bored or do I feel disconnected from the song? Either way, changing pieces can create novelty again.

3. Do I need the Pomodoro method? - Use a little tomato kitchen timer (or your phone) and set it to ten minutes. Tell yourself, "you only have to 'play' for ten minutes" Watch what happens! Many times, after those first ten minutes have passed, you are over the hump and glad to be singing. Also, anytime Toni gets a chance, she has to throw in some Italian. Pomodoro is Italian for tomato.

For this next practice session, we want to go in a little different direction. You may have had a great week, or maybe not. But what we want you to focus on is resilience. When things don't go your way or you have an upsetting event in your life, the way you manage your emotions is imperative. Resilience, when it is built and fine-tuned over time, is a great skill that can make life easier. The great stoic philosopher Seneca said, "We suffer more often in imagination than in reality."

Sing Method

Facing Resistance

S: **Set Your Intention** - How are your emotions affecting your singing life? Are some days easier to sing than others? If so, why? The intention is to simply identify your emotional state.

I: **Isolate From Distractions** - Once you notice any resistance, are you able to identify the feelings which distracted you? Did they cause you to avoid singing? If not, great! If so, how can you navigate those feelings to move past the reluctance?

N: **Notice Your Body** - If you were able to maneuver through the lack of motivation, what sensations did you observe in your body? Where did you feel the resistance? When you take a deep breath and close your eyes, where are those emotions concentrated? Is it in your gut, shoulders, or head? Is it mentally taxing or physically painful?

G: **Give Up Judgment** - The overall goal of this journey is to release judgment and replace it with awareness. If you were able to work through the resistance, allow yourself to feel proud or satisfied that you maneuvered through something that is often very difficult to bypass. As we mentioned earlier, things will not always go as planned. Sometimes we can work through those struggles and other times we need to release our attachment.

Personal Reflection

Celebrate Success: Was I able to sing even when I felt some resistance? Terrific! Did you notice a correlation with why you didn't "feel" like singing? Even if you noticed something as simple as singing after a big meal or being really hungry didn't work well for you, that's worth celebrating. Noticing how your physical or emotional state affects your singing will help you create more success the next time. So keep looking for what helps serve you the most!

Journal Kickstarters:
- Was I here today?
- Was I genuinely present?
- Did I judge myself throughout this time?
- Did I follow through on my intention?
- Did I get distracted by outside activity or the negative thoughts in my head?
- How can I be more consistent with this practice?

Additional Inquiry: This SING Method activity concludes the Battle of the Mind. How did this chapter relate to your personal singing journey? Answer the following questions: Do I need to focus more on releasing judgment, addressing anxiety, or facing resistance? Do I need to forgive someone for their cutting, judgemental words that have held me back from expressing my authentic voice? This is your chance to write about any personal issues in your own battle for the mind. Clear the slate and prepare your spirit for the next chapter.

Chapter Four

Spirit Sets the Tone

Certainly, a book on the mindfulness of singing wouldn't be complete without a chapter on the spirit. We all long for someone to help us transcend and take us on a journey. Twenty years ago, there were very few books on mindfulness and meditation, but today the market is thriving with tools that promote awareness and spirituality. As the world is working through this current post-materialism paradigm shift, individuals are searching for genuine authenticity. What could be more authentic than the human voice?

Perhaps Longfellow says it best, "The human voice is the organ of the soul." You can study with the best teachers and take great care of your body, but if your soul isn't connected, it won't matter. Be brave, bold, and vulnerable enough to share your spirit with someone by singing for them.

Here is a quiz to help you flesh out your spiritual health.
Spirit Quiz - Circle the most appropriate response and assign points as stated below:

>2 points - Agree
>1 point   - Agree Sometimes
>0 points - Disagree

I know my strengths	Agree	Agree Sometimes	Disagree
I know what I'm passionate about	Agree	Agree Sometimes	Disagree
I feel connected to other people outside of my family	Agree	Agree Sometimes	Disagree
Most of the time I feel loved and feel loving	Agree	Agree Sometimes	Disagree
Most of the time I am fearless	Agree	Agree Sometimes	Disagree
I am content most of the time and manage my fear-based thoughts and emotions	Agree	Agree Sometimes	Disagree
I rarely feel drained	Agree	Agree Sometimes	Disagree
I feel I can be myself with my family and co-workers	Agree	Agree Sometimes	Disagree
I have a spiritual practice	Agree	Agree Sometimes	Disagree
I am rarely angry and feel connected to others	Agree	Agree Sometimes	Disagree

Now that you have taken the quiz, what was your score?
- 20 – 14   This is a pretty strong score! Keep going.
- 13 – 7   There are some areas that need to be addressed.
- 6 – 1   You are really hurting, and we suggest you seek some professional help.

Have you ever been deeply moved by a performance during which the singer's overall skill set was not all that great? Maybe they had trouble singing in tune, or the voice sounded a bit harsh and strained; but despite this, you couldn't help but be touched by the performance. Perhaps you even had goosebumps or cried. Why? Because the overall spirit and energy of the performer exceeded their technique. Most individuals will forgive vocal imperfections if the authenticity, heart, and soul of the singer are fully present.

Perhaps you have also had the opposite experience. You may have heard a singer give a technically flawless performance; however, you felt absolutely nothing. Once again, it all comes back to the spirit of the performance. Was the singer so intent on being "perfect" that they missed the soul connection of what they were doing? Some might say the performer simply wasn't in the zone, and others might take a more spiritual approach and say that the heart chakra wasn't fully open.

Fear or Love – Guide the Heart

Addressing the two overarching emotions that drive our spirit is the path to finding our way to presenting authentic, meaningful performances. Psychologists and spiritual teachers often speak about our two core emotions of love and fear. Elisabeth Kubler-Ross sums it up well in this very famous quote.

"There are only two emotions: love and fear. All positive emotions come from love, all negative emotions from fear. From love flows, happiness, contentment, peace, and joy. From fear comes anger, hate, anxiety, and guilt. It's true that there are only two primary emotions, love, and fear. But it's more accurate to say that there is only love or fear, for we cannot feel these two emotions together, at exactly the same time. They're opposites. If we're in fear, we are not in a place of love. When we're in a place of love, we cannot be in a place of fear."

Singing is a practice that calls us to analyze whether we are operating from fear or love. Emotions such as anger, grief, shame, guilt, bitterness, judgment, jealousy, frustration, doubt, and insecurity are all rooted in fear. The "love chapter" in the Bible contains none of those words in reference to the spirit of love. If you have ever had the experience of singing while feeling fear-based emotions, you know it isn't an enjoyable feeling. Who wants to feel afraid while trying to perform a love song? There is a fine line between feeling anger or pain and still being able to sing. If you feel sad and begin crying, it will be nearly impossible to sing. It's a delicate balance of being aware of the emotion and not letting it overtake you. Isn't that the journey of mindfulness and awareness in life? Wouldn't it be awesome to be fully present with our feelings, but instead of being the victim of those feelings, we can be the witness?

Toni was performing in Tel Aviv, and there was an urgent need for her to step in and learn the role of Margherita from Boito's

Mefistofele two weeks before the first performance. We don't recommend waiting until the last minute to learn a role, but sometimes things are beyond our control when an opportunity presents itself. The opera is in Italian, and the role is musically challenging. The other performers were prepared in advance and came ready to sing. She had two weeks to get prepared. Talk about fear! The offer was exhilarating, intimidating, and frightening, all at once. Her thought was, "What the hell do I think I'm doing?" Struggling through the rehearsals was indeed a painful process. After the performance, many people asked where she had performed the role in the states. She laughed and said to herself, "Is that a joke? Are they kidding? I just barely made it through last night, much less other performances!"

The conductor was a woman who had worked with professionals all over the world. The next day she said, "What did you do? It blew me away, and I couldn't sleep because I was wondering what happened." Toni had been so dreadful during rehearsals that she couldn't imagine the performance going well, much less being a great success. "I simply became Margherita!" Toni said. She had such little time to prepare or to think and was so far outside her comfort zone that she had to surrender entirely to the moment, and that's when the magic happened. The magic can happen for you as well.

We wish we could say that after a magical experience, it's possible to live forever in a place of personal freedom and a "zero fear zone." Unfortunately, that isn't how it goes. We often continually look outside ourselves for answers and fail to listen to our own spirit. Our spirit or intuition is talking to us all the time, but we must learn to listen. Remember the *Singers Meditation and Affirmation*, "My intention is to be completely present." Remember the question, "Was I here today?" from your journal exercises. The distraction of emotions, and especially fear, can cause us to not be present during a performance, as well as any other task. Breathwork and meditation are two powerful tools to help us develop and expand our spiritual ritual.

Sing Method

Choosing Love

S: **Set Your Intention** - Choose a song that touches you deeply and helps you get in touch with love based-emotions such as peace, kindness, joy, or gratitude. Experience it fully. See where you can go by allowing yourself to be caught up by the feeling. To be in touch with the emotions of a song is a beautiful form of mindfulness. You may cry for no reason as you sing and let go. This can happen when the emotion of what you are singing triggers a memory or perhaps even a feeling. Go with it. Let the tears flow. This is often a place where singers experience an ecstatic or aesthetic moment. If this happens, consider yourself very lucky indeed.

I: **Isolate From Distractions** - Since you might explore something new in your singing, you may want to bring even more awareness to your surroundings. Try to find an isolated place for this experience. You may feel inhibited if your family is home or you are in a school practice room. You don't want to be preoccupied with what others around you may be thinking.

N: **Notice Your Body** - Was that difficult for you? What did you notice? How did this experience affect your body?

G: **Give Up Judgment** - Perhaps you went so deeply into the emotions that your voice cracked. Good for you! Of course, you don't want that to happen in performance, but the experience can reveal to you where the edge is in expressing emotion without letting it overtake you. It's tricky. Give yourself the grace to explore.

Personal Reflection

Celebrate Success:: If you fully embraced the emotions in a song for the first time, then this is a gigantic win! Was it fun, scary, or exciting? Journal about your most positive takeaway from this activity.

Journal Kickstarters:
- Was I here today?
- Was I genuinely present?
- Did I judge myself throughout this time?
- Did I follow through on my intention?
- Did I get distracted by outside activity or the negative thoughts in my head?

Additional Inquiry: Can I think of times I let fear rule rather than love? When I look back on that experience, what have I learned? Can I give myself grace? Is there a time when someone reacted to me in fear? Can I give them grace?

Breathe - Inhale the Magic

We study and analyze food, exercise, and sleep hygiene, but how often do we explore our own breath? When we are at rest, we breathe an average of 17,000 - 30,000 times a day. So, why would one analyze something that is simple and automatic? Breathwork appears to be one of the hottest new trends in the wellness industry. In 2019, it was a top google search, and that trend has continued to gain momentum. An online search for breathwork will open the door to numerous practices, workshops, and programs in this fast-growing area of interest.

However, breathwork has actually been practiced for centuries in the ancient art forms of tai chi, qigong, and yoga. In the yogic tradition, breathwork is referred to as Pranayama. The common translation of *Prana* is life force and *Yama* is control. However, pranayama is created from an elision (the omission of a sound or syllable when speaking, as in "I'm" and "let's"). The literal word is prana-a-yama. The negative prefix "a" which means to not regulate or to release precedes Yama. Pranayama is thus the releasing or freeing of the life force.

Current scientific research is confirming what mystics and gurus have practiced and explored for centuries: the releasing of a free breath has the power to heal. James Nestor's best-selling book, *Breath: The New Science of a Lost Art*, is a must read.

We found the book to be a riveting journey into the science of breath and felt as though we were traveling right along with Nestor on his trek across the globe witnessing first hand his own fascinating personal experiment with breath. James Nestor said it well, "No matter what you eat, how much you exercise, how skinny or young or wise you are, none of it matters if you're not breathing properly"; and we trust you will breathe better before the end of this book.

The "Breathwork Tool Box" at the end of this section, is based on three powerful types of pranayama which have significant benefits for the voice, mind, body, and spirit. Before sharing these powerful tools, daily habitual breathing patterns must be addressed.

Breathing properly is foundationally important for singing. The goal isn't to provide a physiology lesson or new traditional breathing exercises to improve singing. Our overall goal is to encourage the practice of mindfulness which necessitates stopping and observing breathing habits. What you are doing all day long will significantly impact singing. Here are three questions to help you analyze daily breathing habits:

1. Mouth or Nose?
Nasal breathing versus mouth breathing is a great place to start. There are many doctors and breathwork experts who espouse the benefits of breathing through the nose. As early as 1870, attorney George Catlin wrote an interesting book: *Shut Your Mouth and Change Your Life* based on his transition from mouth breathing to nasal breathing. Nasal breathing also helps fight infections and viruses. As evidenced in Dr. Alan Ruth's article in *Clinical Review*, the health benefits of breathing through the nose versus the mouth are tremendous. Here is a brief summary of some of the health issues attributed to mouth breathing:

- Introduction of unfiltered, poorly humidified air into the lungs
- Upper-chest breathing (inefficient and tiring)
- Chronic over-breathing
- Greater incidence of snoring and sleep apnea
- Bad breath, dental decay, gum disease

He goes on to discuss the benefits of nose breathing; below is a partial list that may help with singing:

- Allows the correct position of the tongue (against the upper palate) and lips (together), assisting the formation of the natural dental arches and straight teeth
- Reduces the likelihood of snoring and apnea
- Warms, moistens, and filters the air
- Helps prevent colds, flu, allergic reaction, hay fever, irritable coughing
- Facilitates inhalation of nitric oxide, a vasodilator and bronchodilator that increases oxygen transport throughout the body
- Keeps some moisture from exhaled air, preventing nasal dryness
- Facilitates correct action of the diaphragm

Breathing with the mouth open during the day is an indication that the mouth is open while breathing at night. An unhinged jaw is great for singing but not for everyday breathing. Working to bring a closed mouth to your awareness may make all the difference. Most people will say they don't sleep with their mouth open, but really there is no way to know for certain. Try this: Tape your mouth at night for a few nights in a row. If you notice feeling better, your mouth is less dry, and your throat is less irritated; you have probably been unaware of your mouth being gaped open at night during sleep. (Don't let your partner find out or they may want to tape it shut all the time.) We thought a little humor here might help because we know how crazy this sounds; but this strategy can really provide great insight into how you sleep.

Ask a friend or loved one to observe your habits. We know, it sounds uncomfortable; but isn't it worth a try if you are exhausted every day from a lack of decent air and sleep? Dr. McKeown, world-renowned author of *The Oxygen Advantage*, as well as many other doctors recommend using 3M Micropore tape which can be removed easily with no pain. If completely covering your mouth gives you anxiety, Dr. McKeown makes a tape that facilitates mouth closure without covering your lips. Your body will thank you with increased energy. There are many issues of mouth breathing that can have an effect on singers.

2. Are you breathing primarily from your upper body (chest) or your lower body (abdomen)?

If you're not sure, try the experiment below:
1. Open your mouth and take a quick breath. What happened to your upper chest? It probably lifted.
2. Now breathe through your nose. Notice the sensation of inhalation is much lower in your body.

Let's try another experiment:
1. Place your right hand on your chest and your left hand on your belly. As you breathe, focus on your right hand.

2. Now take a breath and focus on your left hand. Hopefully, where you placed your attention is where you were expanding.
3. As you go about your day, focus on a Light Slow Deep or an LSD breath. An LSD breath is similar to the sensation one feels when about to go to sleep, as the breath is deep, calm, and quiet. Try to make this part of your daily practice for better respiratory health.

3. How many breaths do you take per minute? (frequency of inhalation)

Now that we have addressed breathing through your nose, with a low quiet breath, let's address the frequency of inhalation. Patrick McKeown, mentioned above, provides the BOLT score as a way of measuring how long one can go without experiencing breath hunger. BOLT stands for Body Oxygen Level Test. By increasing one's bolt score, one can essentially decrease the frequency of breaths per minute. Dr. McKeown states that; "Over the centuries we have altered our environments so dramatically that many of us have forgotten our innate way of breathing. The process of breathing has been warped by chronic stress, sedentary lifestyles, unhealthy diets, overheated homes and lack of fitness. All of these contribute to poor breathing habits." Our modern lifestyle has created a society of chronic over-breathers. He sums it up well, "To oxygenate tissues and organs. We need to breathe less, not more."

We were very honored to have Patrick McKeown on our podcast. On the podcast, he explains the BOLT score and many other helpful topics for singers. To learn more, listen to *Mindfulness of Singing* podcast episode #10. It is available on YouTube or your favorite podcast platform.

When we first read that carbon dioxide is something the body needs, we were really confused because we were taught that carbon dioxide (CO_2) is a waste product of breath and poisonous to our bodies. But in truth, CO_2 is used to break down carbohydrates and proteins in our diet, which creates toxicity and is released through the exhalation process. Additionally, it aids in the oxygenation of our blood cells. We also need CO_2 to help our metabolism. Additionally, the presence of CO_2 informs our brainstem to alert our respiratory muscles and system to breathe and contract. It is when our body has become over-sensitive to CO_2 that we become inefficient breathers.

Have you ever stopped to count how many breaths you take per minute? Pull out the stopwatch feature on your phone. Try to simply observe and not change your current breathing pattern. One way to practice slower breathing is with a breath pacer. Kardia is a free breath pacing app you can download. By watching a circle expand and contract you can guide your breathing to a rate of six breaths per minute, which is the average rate for heart rate coherence. This goal might be too much at first, but the pacer can be adjusted to fit your needs.

We have addressed the very basic components of breathing. After becoming more mindful of your own breath and using an LSD (light, slow and deep) breath, we encourage you to experiment and play with many different types of breathwork practices such as HeartMath Coherence, Oxygen Advantage, Transformational Breath, Buteyko Method, and Wim Hof Method to name a few. Just like meditation, one size doesn't fit all; and the wonder and mindfulness of breathing are just one breath away. The following practices presented in the breathwork toolbox are more advanced and should be used after you have mastered the concept of maintaining a light, slow, and quiet breath first.

Breathwork Toolbox

The breath is truly the engine that is driving the car. It is the power source for the voice. Phonation cannot occur without the breath being put into motion. Yet, breathing is an involuntary response. Unless we practice mindfulness or we are actively involved in breathwork, our subconscious rules our breath. Have you ever noticed your breath follows your emotional state? The beauty of breathwork is that it gives us the ability to change and shift our emotions by changing our breathing. This ability to change our state is one reason breathwork expert Richie Bostock states that "breathing is the body's very own Swiss Army Knife."

Below are three of our favorite pranayama practices, some of our personal experiences with these tools, and specific benefits for the voice, mind, body, and spirit that may be gained as a result of using these strategies. When an adjustment to the flow of your own energy or (prana) is needed, we hope you will stop and remember the powerful toolbox listed below. For a video demonstration of these three practices, go to mindfulnessofsinging.com.

Bhramari
Nadi Shodhana
Kapalabhati

Alternate Nostril Breathing

The blood system is oxidized and prana is brought to the nerves. This pranayama invigorates the entire body, giving alertness to the mind as well. A lightness of the body is produced, the appetite is balanced, and sound sleep results.

The Spiritual Science of Kriya Yoga, Goswami Kriyananda

Sanskrit: Nadi Shodhana - nah-dee shoh-dah-nuh
- Nadi - channel
- Shuddhi - purification

Benefits

Voice - Reduces anxiety, helps ease respiratory allergies that cause hay fever, sneezing or wheezing

Mind - Synchronizes the left and right side of the brain, increases focus

Body - Infuses the body with oxygen, helps balance hormones, clears and releases toxins

Spirit - Balances energy and prepares the body for meditation

Our breath is totally the tour guide for where we are heading. Toni sang with international soprano Lucy Shelton in a live performance broadcast on National Public Radio. Toni was backstage feeling nervous, so she took off one of her shoes, placed her foot in tree pose, and began Nadi Shodhana (alternate nostril breathing) in her gown. She can still remember how transported she felt; she was calm and centered. The performance was wonderful and the evening was exhilarating. A reviewer commented on how equally matched and beautiful their voices were in the duets. Wow! See? She didn't even need yoga pants or a mat to do this exercise, and neither do you! I bet the stagehands had something to talk about for a few weeks.

We are certain that the alternate nostril breathing exercise reduced her anxiety, feelings of intimidation, and helped her have a wonderful evening. For a double whammy, she combined the benefits of alternate nostril breathing and tree pose. Tree pose also helps calm the monkey brain, and she wanted all the help she could get!

Basic Technique for Alternate Nostril Breathing (Nadi Shodhana)

Nadi Shodhana is frequently considered one of the most fundamental pranayama practices because of its ability to synchronize the left and right hemispheres of the brain. Inhaling through the left nostril triggers the rest/relaxation response (parasympathetic nervous system) and inhaling through the right stimulates the fight/flight response (sympathetic nervous system).
Sit on the floor in a crossed leg position or in a chair. It is important to sit with your back erect and your shoulders relaxed and down. If on the floor, sit on a bolster (a small pillow or a folded blanket will also work). This will elevate your hips slightly above your knees and help to maintain proper alignment. If sitting in a chair, make sure not to lean back into the chair. Again, the goal is an erect spine.

Imagine that the spine is a water hose; don't allow any kinks in the hose so that the "water" or air can flow freely.
- Sit comfortably with your spine tall.
- Place the tip of the index finger and the middle finger of the right hand in between the eyebrows.
- Exhale completely.
- Block the right nostril with the thumb and inhale slowly through the left nostril.
- Place the pinky and ring fingers on the left nostril and slowly release the air through the right nostril.
- Keep the ring and pinky finger on the left nostril and inhale slowly through the right nostril.
- Close the right nostril while releasing the left nostril and begin exhaling.
- These two breaths complete one full cycle.
- Repeat for several cycles and gradually increase the number as you feel more comfortable.
- Remember to always inhale through the same nostril you just exhaled through.

For Further Practice

After you are comfortable with the basic pattern of inhalation and exhalation, add a breath-hold at the top of the breath. For example, breathe in through your left nostril very slowly for a count of ten. Imagine the air rising slowly from the pelvic floor up to the top of the head. Close both nostrils and retain the breath for a count of ten. Begin releasing the air from your right nostril very slowly for a count of ten. Imagine the air descending very slowly back down from the top of the head to the pelvic floor while singing.

Put your hands in the air! Pump them twice. Congratulations! You have just practiced breathwork, meditation, AND an element of singing! In singing, there is a retention or holding phase and a slow exhalation phase. It may be useful to incorporate this practice while singing, teaching the body and mind to slow down the breathing process without collapsing the rib cage or over-breathing, as both can be detrimental to the freedom of the voice.

One doesn't need thirty minutes, special clothes, or props to gain the benefits of this excellent pranayama exercise. If one is stressed and simply needs to slow the heartbeat or racing mind, stop for a few minutes and do a few rounds of alternate nostril breathing. Experiment with the number of counts and try increasing the number for each round. As always, listen to the body, play, and enjoy the journey inward.

Skull Shining Breath / Breath of Fire

Brings heat to the body when it is cold. Improves digestion and helps cure asthma and consumption. It also decreases fat, particularly around the stomach area. The benefits are the same as bellows breath.

The Spiritual Science of Kriya Yoga, Goswami Kriyananda

Sanskrit: *Kapalabhati* - Kah-bah-lah-bah-tee
- Kapala - skull
- Bhati – shining

Benefits

> **Voice** - Clears away mucus, increases diaphragmatic and abdominal strength
> **Mind** - Eliminates ruminating thoughts
> **Body** - Improves blood circulation, increases metabolic rate, remove toxins
> **Spirit** - Creates a place of deep meditation and bliss

Toni never stuttered until she went through a stressful event that caused PTSD. Sometimes she could hardly talk as her thoughts and fears were racing. She wished she had been more grounded in pranayama or breathwork practices at the time so that she could have managed and controlled her energy. Since then, she has practiced Kapalabhati, "skull shining breath," or Breath of Fire, and it has helped her tremendously in focusing her intense energy.

In Kapalabhati, exhalation is active, forceful, and fast, while inhalation is passive. This reverses the normal flow of breath as now the exhalation is active and the inhalation is passive. It's important to wait three to four hours after a meal to practice this technique, as it is best to practice on an empty stomach. When comfortable with the breathing practice, it's possible to add a yoga pose to the breath practice.

In Kundalini yoga, there is an exercise called "ego eradicator." In this exercise, one sits in an easy pose for three minutes and practices Breath of Fire while holding the arms up at a 60-degree angle in a V for victory-type posture. The "ego eradicator" has many health benefits, including clearing mucus. Who doesn't need their ego (annoying voice in the head) eradicated while clearing away snot? It's so glamorous!

When Denise was first introduced to the "ego eradicator" she was obsessed with her ability to focus and center after a three-minute session. She introduced her students at the university to this breathwork because of the increasing number of students in her studio suffering from anxiety. She used Breath of Fire with each student before the lesson began. The results were incredible. Not only did the students calm down and were better able to focus, but most of them also began using the technique outside of their lessons, and commenting on their ability to incorporate it into other aspects of their daily lives.

In addition to all the above-mentioned benefits, we both feel that after a round of Kapalabhati breathing, we are in a mental and physical state to practice mindfulness. Go play and enjoy the many benefits of clearing toxins from your body and mind.

Basic Technique for Kapalabhati (Breath of Fire)

Begin in a comfortable, seated position (either in a chair or crossed leg on the floor). Sit with your back erect and shoulders relaxed and down. If in a chair, be sure to sit tall and away from the back of the chair. Again, the goal is an erect spine. Imagine the spine as a water hose through which the "water" or air can flow freely.

- Sit comfortably with the spine tall.
- Place hands on knees with palms open to the sky or in Gyan mudra. (thumb and pointer finger rounded to make a circle)
- Focus the energy only on exhaling as the inhalation will automatically happen when the stomach is released.
- Exhale by pulling in the stomach and drawing the navel towards the spine. In the beginning, it may help to keep the right hand on the stomach in order to feel the abdominal muscles contract.
- Begin with about twenty slow breaths to complete one round of breaths.
- After the round, keep the eyes closed and notice the sensations in the body.
- As you become more comfortable, increase the number and frequency of breaths. Start slowly to develop proper form. Instead of counting the breaths, it's possible to set a timer, gradually working up to three minutes of uninterrupted breaths.

For Further Practice

Add the Kundalini "ego eradicator" mentioned earlier.

- Follow the above steps while holding your arms in a V for victory type posture for three minutes.
- Throughout the practice, keep your pelvic floor muscles active and engaged in mula bandha or root lock. See the following section for more details on mula bandha.
- At the end of the three minutes, intensify the root lock by continuing to contract the pelvic floor muscles for a few seconds and then while your hands are in the air, slowly draw your arms together and allow your thumbs to touch.
- After your thumbs touch, give one last intense squeeze to the pelvic region while stretching your fingers up toward the sky.
- Exhale gradually while slowly allowing the arms to fall to your side (think of pointing your fingers toward the walls) bringing them together in your lap. After this breathing pattern, many people enjoy sitting quietly and relaxing in the wonderful sensation of peace created from their very own breath.

Mula bandha – Beyond kegels! Your partner will thank us!

In yoga, there is a practice of activating and engaging the arches, known as bandhas, in the body. They are also referred to as locks, which can be a bit confusing as the goal is to lift and unlock the different bandhas in the body. The mula bandha, or root lock, helps balance the pelvic floor. Sometimes it is taught as a kegel exercise. Since most people know what a "kegel" is, it may be helpful to use this sensation as a good place to start. However, the lifting and freeing sensation is a bit more subtle than a kegel. Begin by sitting in a comfortable position and imagine bringing the sitz bones (two bony notches on your bottom) together and the pubic bone and coccyx bone together. While doing this, there will be a gentle, lifting sensation in the perineum. Voila! The Mula bandha has been engaged.

Humming Bee Breath

The bee breath produces a most harmonious voice. It cures insomnia. It is an excellent technique for learning concentration.

The Spiritual Science of Kriya Yoga, Goswami Kriyananda

Sanskrit: *Bhramari* - Brah-mah-ree
- Bhramari – Bee

Benefits

Voice - Helps remove excess tension in the vocal cords, helps find a high resonance, and helps lengthen exhalation without strain
Mind - Produces noticeable changes in alpha, theta, and gamma brainwaves
Body - Increases nitric oxide, decreases insomnia, lowers blood pressure
Spirit - Stimulates the pineal gland

The humming bee breath is the only one of these three practices that connects to actual phonation for singing. Judith E. Carman author of *Yoga For Singing* states: "It (humming bee breath) engages the intrinsic muscles of the larynx in a light and smooth way (if done pianissimo and felt at the bridge of the nose rather than loudly and felt in the throat), and it is a beneficial exercise for many purposes."

Sometimes our inability to get started just needs to be sparked with something new. Toni stumbled on Bhramari by accident when she was in one of those low places. The more she practiced this technique, the more she realized its many benefits. Bhramari is a very organic way to practice breathwork, singing, and meditation all at once.

We are not scientists, but we can tell you that humming scales for a few minutes will dramatically slow your breathing and help you get into a meditative state. In *The Oxygen Advantage*, Patrick McKeown explains the science behind this experience: "The production of nitric oxide in the nasal sinuses can be increased by simply humming. In an article published in the *American Journal of Respiratory and Critical Care Medicine,* Doctors Weitzberg and Lundberg described how humming increased nitric oxide up to fifteen-fold in comparison with quiet exhalation. They concluded that humming causes a dramatic increase in sinus ventilation and nasal nitric oxide release."

Scientists and ethnomusicologists agree on the many benefits of bee breath. "Ethnomusicologist Joseph Jordania has theorized that the relaxed, happy feelings elicited by humming may be rooted deep in human evolutionary history. In Jordania's view, humming may once have served the same purpose as animal contact calls—sounds that let animals know that they are among members of their own group, no predators are around, and it's safe to let down their guard and go about their business. Today, humming may still communicate that all is well." *(Psychology Today* by Linda Wasmer Andres)

Studies from the Soft Computing and Intelligent Systems (SCIS) and International Symposium on Advanced Intelligent Systems find that focused vibrations affect alpha, theta, and gamma brain waves. Other studies have shown that depression can be lifted because of these brain wave changes. With all of those positive benefits, we imagine you are ready to buzz like a bee!

Basic Technique for Bhramari (Bee Breath)

Begin in a comfortable seated crossed leg position. Sit with your back erect and your shoulders relaxed and down. You may also choose to sit in a chair. Be sure you are sitting tall and away from the back of the chair. Again, the goal is an elongated spine. Imagine your spine as a water hose so that the "water" or air can flow freely.

- Sit comfortably with your spine straight.
- Close your eyes and your mouth.
- Close the flap of your ears by pressing in gently with your thumb.
- Gently place your index and middle finger over your eyes with the tips resting near the bridge of your nose.
- Rest the ring fingers above the lips, and the pinky fingers below the lips.
- Take a calm, slow inhalation through your nose.
- Exhale slowly while making a soft, gentle, moderately low pitched humming sound like a bee.

- Continue humming for the length of the exhalation.
- Repeat the steps above to complete several rounds of breath.

For Further Practice

Once you are comfortably buzzing on an easy low pitch, begin experimenting with different pitches, and notice the sensations in your body. The goal is always to maintain freedom in your throat. As you go higher, aim for feeling the buzzing sensation in the third eye. This is the area located around the middle of the forehead, slightly above the junction of the eyebrows.

Breathwork Toolbox Summary

We hope that you have not only enjoyed all three of these breathwork practices but have also discovered many things about your voice and breath that will be helpful in moving forward. As you explore these different breathwork techniques, we hope the following quick reference chart will help you address which one is most beneficial. It is an overview of the Breathwork Toolbox for your comparison. For example, if you have mucus or anxiety you can see which practice will address the issue. Remember the guru is in you, and your own breath is your guide to awareness. Happy Breathing!

Benefit	Nadi Shodhana	Kapalabhati	Bhramari
Voice	Reduces anxiety, helps alleviate respiratory allergies that cause hay fever, sneezing or wheezing	Clears away mucus, increases diaphragmatic and abdominal strength	Removes excess tension in the vocal cords, helps find a high resonance and helps lengthen exhalation without strain
Mind	Synchronizes the left and right side of the brain, increases focus	Eliminates ruminating thoughts	Produces noticeable changes in alpha, theta, and gamma brainwaves; excellent technique for learning concentration
Body	Infuses the body with oxygen, helps balance hormones, clears and releases toxins, balances the appetite, promotes sound sleep	Improves blood circulation, increases metabolic rate, removes toxins, brings heat to the body when it is cold, improves digestion, helps cure asthma and consumption, decreases fat, particularly around the stomach area	Increases nitric oxide, decreases insomia, lowers blood pressure
Spirit	Balances energy and prepares the body for meditation	Creates a place of deep meditation and bliss	Stimulates the pineal gland

Sing Method

Discovering Breathwork

***S*: Set Your Intention** - How many minutes will you practice breathwork today? How about tomorrow? Can you do it every day? Try using Kapalbhati (Breath of Fire) before you sing. This will really get your cardiovascular system going.

***I*: Isolate From Distractions** - When you begin your breathwork before you sing, sit down and start slowly. Turn off your phone. Maybe you want to do this outside somewhere, so that family and pets can't interrupt your new practice.

***N*: Notice Your Body** - Breathwork is a rush. You may get lightheaded or experience a slight headache at first; if so, this will subside. Aside from that, do you notice how exhilarated you feel? This is one of our favorite activities of the day. It makes our whole bodies feel so energized.

***G*: Give Up Judgment** - If you can't do Breath of Fire for three minutes, don't worry; you will improve. It's more important to do the sequence slowly, with good form, rather than to rush through. Add 20 seconds each time you explore. You may feel frustrated by your inability to breathe quickly, but this practice will help you have better respiratory health. It will also make your singing better.

Personal Reflection

Celebrate Success: What was my biggest win in this activity? Did I discover a breathwork practice that really resonated with me? Did I feel any resistance and manage to push past that resistance? Go ahead and sing your own praises and celebrate your wins.

Journal Kickstarters:
- Was I here today?
- Was I genuinely present?
- Did I judge myself throughout this time?
- Did I follow through on my intention?
- Did I get distracted by outside activity or the negative thoughts in my head?

Additional Inquiry: How can I incorporate breathwork into my daily routine? Can I schedule a time to explore these practices or other types of breathwork? Can I use breathwork before or after I sing?

Meditation

It's 4:30 a.m.; and as the alarm clock sounds, you struggle to silence the noise and immediately pull the covers over your head. Really? Already? No way, just a few more minutes. Ten minutes pass, and you drag yourself out of bed. No need to get dressed as you were already sleeping in your favorite, comfortable workout clothes. You smooth down your hair a bit just to get rid of the bedhead, quickly brush your teeth so you don't assault anyone with your morning dragon breath, slide into your favorite pair of old worn-out flip-flops, and out the door you go.

Outside you take in the crisp autumn air and shuffle through the fallen leaves, breathing in the stillness and peace all around you. You quietly open the door, grab a thick wool blanket and a bolster as you make your way to the back of the room, hoping you are not taking the spot someone has been sitting in for the last 20 years. At the front of the room, a swami (devotee) briefly plays a singing bowl, and the sequence begins. For the next hour and fifteen minutes, you are transported by chanting in Sanskrit, breathing sequences, and a thirty-minute silent meditation followed by prayers and a closing affirmation.

You have just mentally joined Toni on one of her fall retreats to Yogaville. It's important to notice that the swamis (Sanskrit for "master of one's self" are members of a monastic order,) didn't just walk into the room and immediately began a deep, silent meditation transporting themselves to a place of bliss. Even for these seasoned yogis, there was a sequence of steps to set them up for the long silent meditation. Certainly, we can all experience brief moments of meditation and reflection without a dramatic sequence of prep work. However, if we want to create a meditation practice or take our practice to a deeper level, some personal reflection will help.

Sometimes people simply don't know how to get started with a meditation practice, or they have tried but weren't successful because they couldn't quiet their thoughts. Meditation is not a one-size-fits-all. There are many meditation quizzes online that can help you choose a practice that is right for you. This is the beauty of it; everyone can find a practice that fits perfectly. It's often difficult to shut-off our thoughts. This is very common. If you are new to meditation, we encourage you to find and complete a questionnaire that can help you determine the best practice for you.

Many people enjoy a variety of ways to meditate. The important step here is knowing who you are and what practices may align with you the best. For our purposes, we will discuss six different meditation styles that may interest you. They are:

- Visualization (Observing an object)
- Mantra (Observing a word)
- Self-Inquiry (Observing a question)
- Inner Body (Observing your body)
- Mindfulness (Observing your thoughts)
- Breathwork (Observing your breath)

All the practices we discuss will further encourage the benefits of embracing silence. Sometimes people are surprised by the kind of meditation practice they align with the most. We encourage you to explore them all; the only way to know for sure is to give each one a try.

Toni and I practice different rituals. I am a breathwork meditation person and I use it to relax for sleep. Toni prefers to meditate by taking a mindfulness walk, focusing on a mantra, chanting, or sitting quietly after a breathwork practice. We both like guided meditation (but HATE guided tours or tour guides). Try more than one thing, your experience may surprise you. Even though we both appreciate guided meditation, we enjoy it for different reasons.

Toni appreciates the relaxation of listening to the guide. On the other hand, I like the fact that when I actively listen, my own thoughts will SHUT UP! If it wasn't for the guide, I would write another book in my head. Toni definitely doesn't want that. Visit mindfulnessofsinging.com for a simple, guided, breathwork, meditation.

We encourage you to dive in and explore the following meditation practices. Begin each session by sitting comfortably in a peaceful place. Take your shoes off and relax. If you can lie down without going to sleep, go for it! You can meditate anywhere, but it might be easier if the area doesn't look like a pigpen. Just as we mentioned in preparing a place to practice singing, clutter never creates a calming energy.

Remember how the swami's started their practice early in the morning before it was light outside? This was, for them, an excellent time to meditate. They were working with their bodies' natural rhythms. Find your peak mediation time, and begin each session by taking a light, slow, deep, centering breath; set an intention, and dive into one of the practices below.

You can also add a mudra (muːˈdɹas) to any of the following practices. Mudras are hand gestures or finger postures that convey a specific symbolism or meaning. The Sanskrit translation of mudra is "seal."

While the term mudra is most familiar in Hinduism, Buddhism, and Jainism, one of the most familiar mudras is also found in many of the world's major faith groups. Christians, Jews, and Muslims also use this hand gesture to show the sign of prayer, and in Sanskrit, it is known as Anjali (andʒˈaːli) Mudra. This is also the mudra used when saying "Namaste" (nʌmǝsteɪ). The Sanskrit meaning of Anjali is "to offer" or "salutate"; and as mentioned earlier, mudra means "to seal." It is formed by bringing the palms together in front of the chest, such that the thumbs rest lightly against the sternum. This mudra brings together the left and right hemispheres of the brain and can make us aware of our divine essence.

In India, Namaste is used as a greeting and a sign of respect. In ancient Sanskrit "namah" meant "to bend" and over time it evolved to mean greetings or salutations and the "te" means to you. So literally it means greetings to you.

Yoga communities around the globe have associated the phrase with a much deeper meaning: "the divine light in me sees the diving light in you." This western adaptation of the cultural meaning of simply saying hello can often be rather culturally offensive for some, or it can be a beautiful spiritual practice.

Certainly, the westernization of yoga in many ways is far from its roots, and the adaptation of this phrase outside of its cultural community is just one example.

The Dhyana, (djɑːnə) also known as meditation mudra is performed by sitting in one of two different cross-legged positions. Padmasana, (padˈmɑːsənə) is the cross-legged position in which the legs rest one on top of the other. Sukhasana (suk ɑːsənə), a more simple posture created by the saying criss-cross applesauce. The hands are then placed on the lap, one on top of the other, such that the thumbs touch at the tip. This mudra stills the mind and helps one to build the one-pointed focus which is essential for meditation.

The two mudras mentioned above are the tip of the iceberg. There is a link on mindfulnessofsinging.com, which contains ten of the most popular mudras shared by Deepak Chopra.

As with everything in our book, we view ourselves as simply a guide on your inner exploration. Only you know what resonates best with you. We believe the two simple mudras mentioned above are a great place to start as they both focus on calming and centering the mind, which is certainly beneficial for singers and meditation. You can also incorporate these mudras with the following six meditation practices.

Visualization (Observing an object) A good introduction to visualization is the use of a candle. Focus your eyes on the flame and watch as it dances about. Candles are often used in spiritual practices as symbolism and for the calm feeling they provide. Once you have enjoyed candle meditation, experiment with anything that evokes a feeling of beauty. Mentally, feel it, touch it, smell it. Each time your mind drifts away, gently bring your focus back to the object.

Once you have been able to keep your focus on the object for a while, gradually shift from the object to the peaceful feeling associated with the object. After you are comfortable working with a single object, expand your horizons and mentally travel to your favorite breathtaking view of nature. Close your eyes and "teleport" yourself to whatever peaceful place makes you do a happy dance. To step it up a notch, on every inhalation imagine each cell of your being is saturated with that emotion, and with each exhalation send that feeling out into the world.

Mantra (Observing a word) Mantra is a combination of two Sanskrit words: man - constant thinking and tra - to be free. Thus, the idea of a mantra is to free yourself from constrictive thoughts and ascend to a higher level of consciousness. Perhaps the most famous mantra and the mother of all mantras is Om. The Om mantra is frequently sung and creates an additional benefit for singers. Be aware of the vibration and feel the sense of buzzing on the final M. Don't get too stuck on how many times to repeat the mantra. Some days you will feel compelled to say it more often than other times. Go within and listen to your spirit.

For Catholics, reciting the Rosary is also a powerful form of mantra meditation. While Toni doesn't identify with being Catholic, she has recited the Rosary as a heartfelt form of meditation and has attended beautiful meetings in Italy presented around reciting the Rosary. It's very common now to see people wearing mala bead bracelets and necklaces that are used while reciting a mantra in meditation.

Self-Inquiry (Observing a question) Direct your feelings to a question and observe your feelings. Quiet the ego and aim for the answers that lie deeper inside you. We have all had the experience of "auto-pilot" when driving on a familiar road. You suddenly snap out of it and realize you weren't even aware of the drive. Sometimes you are in deep thought or fantasy. You may even come up with great ideas or solve a problem along the way. We are not asking you to drive and meditate! And don't recommend this habit.

However, self-inquiry is a bit like this experience in that you aren't talking to someone or racking your brain trying to come up with an answer. It is like something appearing in the landscape as you drive. You get in a zone, and the answer just comes.

Inner Body (Observing your body) Chakras are energy centers along the spine. The goal of this practice is to observe the seven different chakras or energy centers of the body. Notice each center and observe if there is any tension in relation to that specific chakra. Some energy centers need to be energized and upregulated, and some need to be relaxed and downregulated.

Mindfulness (Observing your thoughts) The goal is simply to observe your thoughts without placing any judgment upon them. It's as if you are sitting outside of yourself and watching. This practice involves activating all of your senses and being fully present. This is the complete opposite of the driving experience mentioned earlier. With mindfulness, you are completely aware of everything on the drive.

Breathwork (Observing your breath) See the previous section and the Breathwork Toolbox found on our website. Breathwork is the remote control for changing and controlling our emotional state. Your power to change is only one breath away!

Now that you have a bit more understanding of each of these meditation techniques, don't let any excuses get in the way of delving into something new. People will make up excuses for anything they don't really want to do. We often hear people say, "I'd like to start a diet but..." or "I'll do my taxes when..." We all make excuses about things we know we should do. But truthfully, excuses don't move you forward. Everyone around you is tired of hearing the excuses, including yourself. There's that sword of truth! Hurts doesn't it?

Remember, it is important not only to hear the truth but also respond with kindness. Having self-compassion is key. When you see a shortcoming, acknowledge it, and then move on. In fact, it could be something on which you meditate. Ask yourself: why are you resistant?

If you are a meditation aficionado skip this part and go to the next SING Method.

If you are stuck, keep reading. The following list will help you see those excuses for what they really are — lame. Do the arguments below resonate or sound familiar to you?

It sounds boring

1. It is a first, but then you will appreciate the practice of sitting down and relaxing for a few minutes every day.
2. Have you tried listening to binaural beats or guided meditations? Not boring.

I can't sit still.
  1. Look at that! We have something in common! Sitting still is something you can learn. You will get better at it after a while.
  2. Try doing a form of meditative yoga.

I don't have time.
  1. We are going to call bullshit on that. Look at your phone screen time. Need we say more?
  2. Start with five minutes a day. You can find all kinds of meditations that are only five minutes long.
  3. Set your alarm a few minutes early to take advantage of a quiet morning. This may help you start the day with a new positive habit.

I don't like to try new things by myself.
  1. Find a friend who has always talked about trying it too.
  2. Find a friend who already practices, and ask if they can help.
  3. Download an app, and think of it as your friend.
  4. When you feel more comfortable, join a group in your area that practices.

My mind won't slow down.
  1. Again, us too! But if you don't pay any attention to it, after a while it quiets down and you will be able to let all those thoughts float by.
  2. No one is keeping score, so don't worry about it.

Meditation makes me sleepy.
  1. Maybe you need it; go with it, take a nap.

2. Try a little tea beforehand, it will help to wake you up a bit.

Meditation is hard.
1. Yes, it is. Not even going to lie, but we can assure you it is worth every minute of sticking with it to get better at the practice.
2. Anything worth doing is challenging and difficult at first.
3. If your environment does not allow for quiet time, consider taking part in a class. This will improve your chances of success by providing a supportive community.

If you still aren't convinced, there are some scientific studies that should get you over the hump. Several studies have shown meditation to reduce stress. Meditation decreases the stress hormone cortisol which produces harmful effects within the body and causes inflammation. All of those processes would certainly be detrimental to the singer. Even if a singer enjoys singing, they can sometimes struggle with stage fright (which is a form of fight or flight), and meditation is a way to bring down the stress hormone created when one is performing. The production of this flight or flight hormone can disrupt sleep, make one feel depressed, increase blood pressure, and can contribute to brain fog.

We don't know about you, but we are happy to meditate if it means sleep improves. Plus, cortisol creates fat around your middle. You know, the kind that raises the likelihood of having a heart attack or a stroke. Who is interested in having a stroke and needing someone to change their diapers? We will meditate every hour if it means we can avoid that nightmare.

Literally hundreds of studies have been done about the effects of meditation and mindfulness practices. Studies have been completed covering a broad spectrum of issues such as PTSD, various phobias, children in inner-city war zones, terminally ill,... the list goes on. All of these diverse situations show positive outcomes from the effects of meditation on the brain and neurology. In fact, Patrick McKeown states that 75% of those suffering from anxiety and panic disorder have dysfunctional breathing. That's another great reason to sit down, slow down, and observe your breathing as a form of meditation.

Here's another story. We have mentioned that Denise has stenosis of the spine. There is nothing like back pain; it has a special suckiness. When she was in the worst pain, she could not tolerate massage or much of anything that was supposed to relieve it. But one day she heard Sam Harris, a meditation guru, talk about how pain is the dreading of the next moment; and that if you can embrace it and breathe, you can get through the experience with little or no feeling of actual pain. His premise is that the mind has everything to do with our reality and that pain is a construct. Sounds woo-woo, we know.

One day she wanted to try out a new masseuse and went to a little shop where a Chinese lady owns the "spa." She made an appointment and went in for her massage. They walked back through a dark hallway and heard someone screaming and cursing at the top of her lungs. Fear set in. But she had already paid the bill and didn't want to appear to be a chickenshit, so she stayed. She took off her clothes and got on the table. The masseuse promptly got on top of the table; and using her elbows, she dug in. OMG!!!!

Denise thought she was going to pass out. That lady screaming next door was enduring the same torture. She immediately thought, "no way am I screaming like that," but she wanted to. She wanted to curse, scream, and throw that little lady across the room. Then she remembered what Sam Harris said.

She began "embracing the pain" and stopped actively dreading what the masseuse might push on next. To her surprise, it was how she got through that massage without screaming her head off. The pain came and went depending on how focused she was. When she was not dreading the hot force the lady used to push her flesh practically through the table, and chose to focus on embracing the pressure, the pain was lessened. She learned that day that pain is a construct, and that if she had gone to the masseuse regularly, she may have increased her tolerance to that "feeling" of intense pain. Since then, she has used this mental exercise to deal with headaches, back pain, a bruised toe, a burn on her hand, and cold weather. It works. Wouldn't you like to change the way you react to the pain and the negativity life can throw at you? OM...

On a side note, learning to embrace pain and negativity is one of the aspects of hormesis. Hormesis can be defined as good stress; or as Nietzsche stated, "That which doesn't kill us makes us stronger." The key to hormetic stress is that it needs to be in small increments. Plunging into arctic waters for a long time could be deadly, but a cold shower will actually stimulate the immune system. Other examples include exercise, sunlight, fasting, and exposure to extremes of both hot and cold temperatures. Significant research shows that meditation helps regulate body temperature and breath rate when one is putting the body into hormesis. Meditating can take the dread and fear out of the process.

The scientific benefits alone are compelling enough to start a meditation practice; but have you ever stopped to consider that meditation is a spiritual component of every major organized religion? Meditation isn't actually a modern new-age technique. It has been around for centuries. It's only considered "new-age" because there is a rebirth in awareness of it. Science can now prove with measurable certainty the experiences that mystics from all religions have known for centuries.

"In 2001, researchers at the University of Pavia in Italy gathered two dozen subjects, covered them with sensors to measure blood flow, heart rate, and nervous system feedback then had them recite a Buddhist mantra, the original Latin version of the rosary, the Catholic prayer cycle of the Ave Maria, which is repeated half by a priest and half by the congregation. They were stunned to find that the average number of breaths for each cycle was 'almost exactly' identical, just a bit quicker than the pace of the Hindu, Taoist, and Native American prayers: 5.5 breaths a minute." James Nestor, *Breath: The New Science of a Lost Art*

If you are not interested in religion, that doesn't rule you out either. Your meditation practice doesn't have to be attached to any particular religion; and yet, if it makes it a richer experience for you to associate your meditation practice with your faith, go for it!

There are sacred texts addressing meditation found in Hinduism, Buddhism, Judaism, Christianity, Islam, and many other faith groups. For Christians, the Bible has many Psalms exhorting one to meditate. Many believe that Jesus' 40 days and 40 nights in the wilderness were spent in meditation listening to the voice of God. As a Jew, Jesus would have been exposed to a rich heritage of meditation practices. Paul in his letter to the Philippines admonishes the faithful to renew their minds by meditating on what is good. One might view this as a form of mantra meditation.

Finally, brothers, whatever is true, whatever is noble, whatever is right, whatever is pure, whatever is lovely, whatever is admirable—if anything is excellent or praiseworthy—think about such things.

Philippians 4:8

With a rich sacred tradition and many scientifically proven benefits, meditation is a free and beautiful path to enrich one's journey of mindfulness. We have given you a great deal of information; but you don't need to absorb everything at once, just begin right where you are!

Let's apply all of these meditation benefits to singing, one of the most ancient forms of healing. Mothers have been singing to soothe their babies since the beginning of man. The "new age" concept of sound healing has been practiced for centuries in group chanting. Let's use meditation as a way to practice the art of singing.

Sing Method

Exploring Meditation

***S*: Set Your Intention** - What meditation practice would be most beneficial for you? Plan when you will explore your meditation practice. Ideally, it would be great to plan meditating before you sing.

***I*: Isolate From Distractions** - Gather whatever materials you might need: candle, guided audio, etc. As with most meditation practices, when one first begins it is difficult to quiet the mind. When you get distracted, go back to your breath or a mantra you have chosen. Don't let being distracted distract you! Remember, learning to meditate is a discipline that takes time.

***N*: Notice Your Body** - Observe how you feel before, during, and after your meditation. If you paired your meditation before your singing, did you notice any improvement in your concentration while you were singing? If you hummed, sang, or chanted, did you notice the voice being more warmed-up? Was this order beneficial, or did meditating first make you too relaxed to practice? If so, flip them around. The order is not important. Find what works best for you.

***G*: Give Up Judgment** – If you didn't have some grand "ah ha" moment, it doesn't mean that the practice isn't a match, or that you can't meditate. All new meditators struggle at first with the feeling of failure. Give it another try. If you continue to explore the same meditation and it doesn't resonate with you, go back to the list as there are many options!

Personal Reflection

Celebrate Success: What did I enjoy most about my meditation experience? What did I find helpful or easy? If you meditated for the first time or the 100th time, celebrate your experience.

Journal Kickstarters:
- Was I here today?
- Was I genuinely present?
- Did I judge myself throughout this time?
- Did I follow through on my intention?
- Did I get distracted by outside activities or the negative thoughts in my head?
- How can I be more consistent with this practice?

Additional Inquiry: What meditation style is my favorite and why? Are there any sensations that are new to me? What meditation style will I explore next?

Singer's Five Love Languages

We began the topic of spirit by stating that everything we do is rooted in fear or love. Perhaps new or improved breathwork and meditation practices will give you further insights to your own motivations of fear and love. Denise has playfully teased me, Toni, over the years about my hesitancy to say yes. I mentioned earlier that she is the idea-queen. Whatever it is, she has a full throttle attitude of "we should do "XYZ!" I, on the other hand, tend to respond with, "... well,... maybe." The root of my maybe response is motivated by uncertainty and fear. "What if I can't? Maybe I shouldn't. What if I fail? What will people think?" etc. It might look like I am pouring cold water on her ideas, but in reality her ideas are frequently nudging up to my own insecurities.

I always assumed that Denise's "yes" to everything attitude came from a place of absolute confidence. We were well into writing this very book, when she surprised me by saying that the root of her "yes" response was also driven by fear. What?! She revealed that her underlying drivers of fear were, "What if I get left out? - I'll be insignificant if I don't." etc. All this time I was clueless that fear could actually be part of her subconscious programming as well. Her fear simply revealed itself completely differently than mine did to me.

There is an exercise of answering the question; "Who are you really?" The process is completed once the individual has given all the standard responses of relationship titles, job titles, hobbies etc, and the individual has no words left to describe themselves. Then the person is asked, "What are you afraid of?" After they have exhausted their fears, the facilitator asking the questions states, "This is who you really are." Our titles may define us, but what drives and shapes us are our fears. In regard to your own singing voice, what motivates you: fear or love?

There is a concept of parenting your inner child, but how about parenting your inner singer? What love language does your inner soul hear most effectively?

The Five Love Languages: The Secret to Love That Lasts by Gary Chapman was written to help couples communicate and express love to each other more clearly. If one individual's love language is "words of affirmation," but their spouse's language is "tangible gifts," they may experience a failure to communicate love effectively. There is nothing worse than being given a pair of golf shoes when all you wanted was to have the dishes done. A good friend once asked Denise what she wanted for her birthday, and Denise replied, "I would like that piece of furniture painted black." Her friend said "Huh?" You see, he is a handy guy who builds and has a side gig of being a subcontractor, so she knew it was in his skill set. Now, she has a beautiful black piece of furniture in her home. You never know what you will get, if you are brave enough to ask.

Armed with your personal breathwork and meditation tools, we hope you will dive fully into the following exercise and embrace whatever comes up for you. Are you trying to motivate yourself and your voice with fear or love? Has your inner singer missed your own way of expressing love to yourself? How much do you love your voice? What love language are you using to express love to your inner singer? Which one of these singer's love languages resonates with you the most? See if your inner child does a "happy dance" to one of these ideas.

Gifts - Does your voice need to be loved by honoring it with a tangible gift or investment in its value? Here are some ideas: Purchase music for the song you have been dying to sing. Buy A Singing Straw (see our website to buy one) to soothe and pamper your voice, or maybe you could use a pitch pipe to sing on the go. If your budget allows, maybe it's time to upgrade your piano, take voice lessons, or buy a great microphone for recording that gorgeous voice inside you. It is important to honor your talent and voice by being willing to invest in yourself. Tell your voice it matters, with a gift that speaks *love* to you.

Quality Time - Love your voice by giving some quality time to whatever would recharge your battery the most. When was the last time you sang just for fun? Schedule a singer's date with yourself! Nope, you can't sing anything you "have to work on" for performances, lessons, etc. Would you be inspired to attend a concert in a genre you don't normally embrace? Could the concert, video, etc. be a quality time of investment and inspiration for your voice? How about spending time with your voice and other like-minded people by joining a community choir? Singing with a community is great for your soul and sense of well-being.

Acts of Service - Maybe the best way you could show love to your voice is by valuing it enough to share it with someone else. Sometimes the gigs that are the most rewarding don't come with a big paycheck. Maybe combining your talents with your passion for a specific cause or charity would be an awesome and fulfilling way to show your own love and value to your voice. Perhaps you could give your gift to an assisted living community or for a group of special needs adults or children. Giving back to your community is also very rewarding and touches the lives of those around you. For a great example of incorporating singing with acts of service, go to athousandhandsamillionstars.com, a powerful collaborative project by Denise.

Words of Affirmation - How about a love letter to your voice? Perhaps there is something you and your voice need to have a chat about. Have you forgiven yourself for some little or big trauma in relation to your voice? Maybe now would be a good time to write a letter of forgiveness to yourself about the incident. How about showing some love to yourself by writing five unique things about your voice? As we mentioned, earlier there is magic in writing. Give yourself some love with your own personal words of affirmation.

Touch - Since our voice isn't literally just our larynx, how about placing one hand over your heart, and one hand on your belly, and sitting in a place of gratitude for the ability to simply phonate. It's a gift we frequently take for granted until we lose our voice and are reminded of how precious it is to communicate. You can also give yourself a laryngeal massage. This is a safe and awesome way to ease tension and help the larynx set in a low position.

Basic Technique for Laryngeal Massage
1. Grab your favorite massage oil or lotion.
2. Put the lubricant on your thumb and forefinger.
3. Make a hand gesture like you are turning a key.
4. Separate the thumb from the rest of the hand.

5. Place your fingers on each side of the larynx just under the jaw.
6. Gently move your hand down toward your chest and then release and start back up at the top of the larynx.

This is a very relaxing and soothing massage technique. Enjoy!

Sing Method

Loving Your Voice

S: **Set Your Intention** - Read back through the five suggestions of how to show love to your singer's soul, and choose one that speaks to you. Was there one that jumped out at you when you first read through the original list? Set a designated time in your calendar when you will experiment with this activity.

I: **Isolate From Distractions** - Don't allow other people or activities to get in the way of your date with yourself. Sometimes we self-sabotage by allowing ourselves to be distracted by others or by not being able to say no. Remember, sometimes it is hard to show yourself love and respect. We think of all kinds of ways to not respect our voices, often because we don't think we deserve it. Kick those thoughts to the curb and go out and give your voice some lovin'.

N: **Notice Your Body** - Take a few centering breaths before you explore the activity. Bring awareness to your body and reflect on how you feel before and after this personal expression of love to your voice.

G: **Give Up Judgment** – Resist the urge to set any preconceived ideas of where you think the activity should take you.

Personal Reflection

Celebrate Success: Did I honor my voice? Did it feel good to show some love to my singer soul? What did I learn from this activity? Sometimes the person we neglect to love the most is ourselves. Celebrate any attempt to honor your voice.

Journal Kickstarters:
- Was I here today?
- Was I genuinely present?
- Did I judge myself throughout this time?
- Did I follow through on my intention?
- Did I get distracted by outside activities or the negative thoughts in my head?
- How can I be more consistent with this practice?

Additional Inquiry: Are there other ways I need to show more respect for my voice? Have I ever thought about loving and honoring my individual voice?

Embracing the Silence

The ability to listen is crucial for singing. Embracing silence can improve our ability to listen, recalibrate our ears to the surrounding sounds, and improve our hearing.

Many scientific articles are addressing the fact that increasing noise pollution is having a negative impact on our health and well-being. When you add the external noise pollution all around us to the cacophony of sounds in our head, that's a lot of chatter we are constantly trying to tune out. Embracing the silence gives us a chance to slow down and stop fighting the noise. For singers, this ability to quiet the clamor both externally and internally gives us a chance to recharge. Thus, our whole instrument can function more effectively. Developing the discipline that is required to quiet the mind and sit in silence can heighten and enhance the same discipline it requires for shutting out the negative voices that pop-up when we are singing or practicing.

One discipline in the realm of therapy is to sit in silence with someone when they are working on themselves or a problem. The counselor who can hold space and just sit with a client can elicit more change than one who gives advice or explains. Sometimes it would behoove the voice teacher to just sit quietly and let a student keep singing or talking until they have their own ah-ha moment.

If you want to truly know who you are, turn off the peripheral noise. Go to a quiet place and spend time alone. Even better, take your own personal silent retreat. There are many different types of spiritual centers that offer personal retreats. Toni has enjoyed staying in monasteries in Italy and ashrams in the states. Often, you don't have to be a member of a particular faith group to enjoy the serenity of a spiritual location. Monasterystays.com offers off-the-beaten-path locations and a more economical way to travel. Il Santuario della Madonna della Guardia di Genova is nestled high in the mountains of northern Italy, not too far from Milan. Yes, the rooms will be sparse and perhaps more rustic than you're used to, but the view will be absolutely spectacular, and you will be treated to a wonderful experience.

You might also plan a getaway to recharge in the beauty of creation. Once, when Toni faced a very difficult crossroads event in her life, she visited Earthwalkways.com near Fredericksburg, Virginia. The facility provided a safe place for her to camp completely by herself, deep in the forest surrounded by a beautiful stream. She could fast and pray for four days. Each day Darlene, the wise owner of the facility, would check in with her in the woods. It was truly a yin-yang experience filled with beauty and pain.

During this time, she was also without a watch or a phone. A clock or time fast is an eye-opening experience. Unplugged from our human constructs of time, we realize just how bound to time we are in our everyday lives. Even though Toni had nowhere she needed to go, nothing to cook, and no one to see, her brain was programmed for wanting to know the time. She realized that nature provides us a clock, if we can slow down long enough to truly listen. In the stillness within, she found the answers she needed by sitting quietly in nature. She learned how to pause.

Practice the pause. Pause before judging. Pause before assuming. Pause before accusing. Pause whenever you're about to react harshly and you'll avoid doing and saying things you'll later regret.

Lori Deschene

Silence may also enable you to find peace and, hopefully, yourself. When we sit in silence, we hear things we otherwise wouldn't, and our desires become apparent. Silence is a necessity. Just as we need to eat, practice good hygiene, sleep, exercise, and go to work, we need time in our day to practice silence, so that inner knowledge of what's important to us carries into our daily actions. This can give us peace even in stressful circumstances. We find contentment in the knowledge that we are everything we need. Silence helps bring us back to a place of rest and clarity within, away from the noise of the world and our own subconscious programming.

We may be afraid of silence; we want to be heard and seen, and often equate silence with insignificance. This is why when we post something on our social media feed we check it over and over to see how many likes or reactions we get. When there isn't enough feedback, we feel small. No wonder our children have developed so much anxiety. Everyone wants to be relevant. We want to be important. This desire can be very strong. But in our pursuit of significance, we often shut out our inner voice. Yet, it is our inner voice that we need to hear the most, not our subconscious programming or the programming we receive through advertisement and social media.

In relation to embracing silence, now might be a good time to assess your overall social media health. *The Social Media Dilemma* is an excellent documentary that might help you evaluate whether you have a social media addiction. If the news feed from everyone else is the very first thing you must consume to start your day or the last thing you insist on doing before going to bed, what priority are your own thoughts in programming your day?

What we don't realize is that we are looking for something we already possess. The peace that we think others will give us by making us feel important is not out in the ether, or in the hands of someone else, it is in the present — the moment we have within us. We are like fish in the pond searching for water or birds in the sky longing for air, and all of our searching keeps us from seeing the obvious.

Sing Method

Welcoming Silence

***S*: Set Your Intention** - If you currently aren't in a position to create a retreat similar to the examples mentioned above, start right where you are! Can you spend 15 minutes alone in silence (without your phone)? In this application, the focus is primarily on listening rather than singing. However, if you can sing a little after the activity, that would be a terrific way to notice how silence affects your ability to slow down and concentrate better when you sing.

***I*: Isolate From Distractions** –If nature speaks to you, we highly encourage you to embrace your silence in nature. If the weather is appropriate, take your shoes off, and enjoy some grounding, and get some sunshine as well.

***N*: Notice Your Body** –Is the thought of this exercise making you squirm with trepidation, or is your spirit doing a happy dance for some me-time? When you spend time in silence, how does the body inform you of the effects? Are you anxious or relaxed? Does your breathing slow down or speed up? If you wear a tracker, what was your heart rate or your variable heart rate? What do these messages from the body tell you?

***G*: Give Up Judgment** –If this is new to you, it might surprise you how difficult or easy the activity is for you. If this was a struggle, be curious. We can't stress enough the importance of bringing curiosity to each of the SING Method practices. The same curiosity you have about embracing or hating the silence might create amazing awareness when you sing.

Personal Reflection

Celebrate Success: Did I have an "ah ha" moment, or a positive experience, before, during, or after the silence? Many people are terrified of silence. If you tried this experience, that's worth celebrating!

Journal Kickstarters:
- Was I here today?
- Was I genuinely present?
- Did I judge myself throughout this time?
- Did I follow through on my intention?
- Did I get distracted by outside activities or the negative thoughts in my head?
- How can I be more consistent with this practice?

Additional Inquiry: What can I do to enrich this experience? Do I need more distance from others to fully embrace the silence? Where will I have my next adventure in silence? This is the final SING Method for Spirit Sets the Tone. Is there anything you know holding you back from allowing your spirit to be totally free in singing?

Chapter Five

Body as the Instrument

We have often thought that instrumentalists are truly lucky since they don't have to carry their instruments everywhere they go. There is never a time when a singer's instrument isn't with them. This means that the mindfulness of the body is critical for the care of the singer's voice. The care given to daily habits can significantly impact the singers' success when singing.

A car owner must make certain the car has oil, water, rotated tires, fuel and is driven regularly. Without this maintenance regimen, the car will eventually break down and the investment is lost. Though many people would never neglect their car, they may neglect the care and maintenance of their body, which is far more valuable than any car you could ever own. Yes, even more valuable than a Bugatti. Just ask the person who has health problems. They will tell you that health is the most important thing in the world.

Why do we often neglect the one thing that can make or destroy our life as we know it?

One can also experience the kind of loss to the voice that is created over time by ignoring proper care and maintenance of the body. Singers in midlife may notice a difference in their voices around the time of menopause or as they age. This is covered in depth in the highly acclaimed book *Singing Through Change: Women's Voices in Midlife, Menopause, and Beyond* by Bos, Bozeman, and Frazier-Neely. There is a lot of research regarding voice and age-related changes for both males and females. Additionally, health and wellness can affect the stamina of breath and other voice-related issues. Sometimes addressing these various health concerns can have an amazing impact on the voice. After all, the body is the instrument.

When Denise was in her early 30s, she took a group of people on a skiing trip to Keystone, Colorado and had an accident. The recovery was long and hard. During her recovery, she realized that a healthy body is truly a gift. She could have been offered money, trips around the world, passion, romance - you name it - and she would have said no. All she wanted was her healthy, fully functioning leg back.

Because of Denise's back problems, she was desperate to change what the doctors told her. "A spinal fusion of four vertebrae in two weeks." Those were words she would not take lying down. So, she read as many books as she could about inflammation and joint health. This put her on a regime of supplements, breathwork, moving more, and cutting out foods that cause inflammation. These changes altered the trajectory of not only her spinal health, but also her health overall.

She was very surprised, when contracted to sing Handel's *La Resurrezione* (which is very high and requires great agility), that she could sing it with ease. What had made her singing so much easier than a year ago? It hit her, "I have been changing my entire body, and it has affected my instrument!" Duh! The elimination of foods that cause an inflammatory response, the addition of supplements, and the work to increase breath stamina reversed what many consider the inevitable changes that come with aging. Bull-Hockey!

Denise was so inspired by this, that she wanted to know if other singers would have the same outcome. She then conducted a 16-week study under the guidance of an orthopedic surgeon. The study was to discover if age-related voice problems could be reversed or slowed down. We are big believers that we don't have to accept everything the medical community tells us about aging.

The study focused on people who were experiencing problems related to voice (speech and singing), such as respiration function, range, predictability of voice quality, and lack of vocal flexibility. These issues are often associated with aging. The intention of the study was to discover whether a holistic health approach could impact the loss of vocal resiliency.

The study consisted of four pillars: (1) Anti-inflammatory Diet, (2) Supplements purported to help with connective tissue, (3) Walking and movement - at least 10,000 steps a day, and (4) Breathwork and respiration interventions.

The pillars were stacked, as the participants continued the protocol. In other words, as they introduced each new pillar, the participants did not stop the previous element. By the end of the study, they would have been doing all four pillars for three weeks. By implementing each one separately, it was hoped the participants could document how they felt and could identify which part of the protocol was helping or, perhaps, not impacting their health.

The initial protocol was to get a good baseline of vocal range, flexibility, and breath control. Participants were to document the notes on each end of their range from the highest note to the lowest note, disregarding whether they sing them publicly.

They were also asked to log how long they could hold a note in the bottom, middle, and top of their range. They also logged how long they could sing a phrase of music. This required them to disregard rests and empty measures to test whether they could sing extended phrases before running out of air.

To measure vocal flexibility, we asked them to log how quickly they could sing a phrase that required vocal agility and to document the degree of difficulty. Participants notated their results on a scale of one to ten, with "1" being "super easy" and "10" representing "very difficult."

Once the singing baseline was created, we wanted to have documentation of their overall cardiovascular and respiratory health. We asked them to track how long it takes them to walk at a comfortable pace for two miles. We also asked them to get a BOLT score.

The final preliminary information we requested was recent blood work, so a baseline could also be recorded. If they were on any medication, we asked them to check with their health care providers because we would be introducing certain supplements during the study.

The first week of the study the participants were asked to stop eating certain foods that cause things such as GERD or acid reflux, inflammation in the body, brain fog, and achy joints.

We also asked that they walk two miles daily. We asked them to shorten the time needed to complete those miles every day, even if it was just by two or three minutes.

Each week we asked them to complete the following survey:

---

1. Have you been able to follow the food protocol every day? If not, how many days have you been able to follow it?

Rate the following questions on a scale from 1 to 10, (1 being no difference, 10 being completely different):

2. How has your digestion improved? _____
3. How has your energy improved? _____
4. How has your range improved? _____
5. How has your sleep improved? _____
6. What is your highest note? _____
7. What is your lowest note? _____
8. How long can you hold a note? _____
9. What is the longest phrase you can sing? _____
10. Please record your BOLT score: _____

We could go into the mean scores and data, but we thought it would be more interesting for you to read the comments people wrote each week. Here is what they said:

Week 2:
- Energy up!
- Less bloated, constipation less severe, wake up less, more energy
- Bloating gone-flat abdomen!
- Energy way up-less brain fog

Week 4:
- Sleeping better & improved BOLT score
- I have lupus so energy is low, but digestion is better
- Stomach less bulky
- Sleep better
- Better BOLT

Week 8:
- Sleep has improved
- Better BOLT
- Sleeping better, energy up and tummy is happier

Week 12:
- Changes are dramatic
- Diet changed by daily wellbeing
- My voice is back to life
- Really dramatic changes

If you are interested in *The Healthy Voice Protocol*, you can go to our website and request the guide. We will happily send it to you!

There are two mindsets about health: one is that aging is inevitable and brings illnesses, weakness, and pain. The other is, that with proper care, awareness, knowledge, and maintenance, the aging process doesn't have to be debilitating, keeping you from living a full life. We have all seen on Instagram and other social media posts about people in their 80s and 90s dancing, working out, singing (really well too) and enjoying themselves. So, it is possible. There is living, walking proof all around us.

If you long to experience changes in your vocal health and ability, we encourage you to embrace this chapter and be honest in this upcoming assessment. Do your best to take the quiz and get a baseline of where you are now.

The following is a singer's health awareness questionnaire. These areas have a profound and significant impact on one's ability to sing. As you take this quiz, remember that no one is watching, and there is no final grade. Being truly honest with yourself just might bring about some positive changes. Dive in and let the transformation begin! We hope you take this chapter very seriously.

Body Quiz - Circle the most appropriate response and assign points as stated below:

    2 points - Agree
    1 point - Agree Sometimes
    0 points - Disagree

I like my body	Agree	Agree Sometimes	Disagree
I have loads of energy	Agree	Agree Sometimes	Disagree
I eat healthy foods	Agree	Agree Sometimes	Disagree
I have alcohol and caffeine in moderation	Agree	Agree Sometimes	Disagree
I always feel good in my clothes	Agree	Agree Sometimes	Disagree
I get plenty of sleep and feel awake all day	Agree	Agree Sometimes	Disagree
I have been to the doctor in the last year for a checkup	Agree	Agree Sometimes	Disagree
I get some form of exercise every day	Agree	Agree Sometimes	Disagree
I eat a well-balanced diet of protein fruit and veggies	Agree	Agree Sometimes	Disagree
I use good oral hygiene each day	Agree	Agree Sometimes	Disagree

Now that you have taken the quiz, what was your score?

- 20 -14   This is a pretty strong score! Keep going.
- 13 - 7   There are some areas that need to be addressed.
- 6 - 1   You are really hurting, and we suggest you seek some professional help.

Hydration - Aqua Vita

The brain, which is comprised of about 70 percent water, accounts for around two percent of the body's weight but uses 20 percent of the body's energy and oxygen. Thus, any level of dehydration impairs the brain. Hydration is also crucial for the vocal folds to stretch and move with ease when singing. Once a person feels thirsty, dehydration has already set in. By the way, coffee, alcohol, pop, and sugary drinks do not count towards hydration efforts. Drinking coffee and alcohol can also have a drying effect on the vocal cords, so use sparingly.

I have often wondered why my body needs as much water as Toni's. She is tall and athletic in her build, and I am short and, well, not athletic (and I am ok with it... ish). As someone who struggles with drinking enough water without constantly needing a bathroom nearby, I can tell you, good hydration can present a problem. Recently, I ran across a study that says water from the tap does not hydrate like it should; neither does bottled water. Water should have electrolytes present and should also have a balanced alkaline composite.

Fancy bottled electrolyte water can be expensive and put more plastic in the environment. Instead, you can buy a glass water bottle, invest in a filter, and then add some essential minerals. You can purchase about a month's supply of essential minerals on Amazon for very little. This essential mineral water cuts down on bathroom visits, as well. In addition, you may have fewer headaches and your skin may be less dry. Perhaps you've heard the saying "pee pale," which is good advice; but also remember that peeing less is good too. If you are drinking plenty of quality water, your body will use it for cellular activities, thus, holding on to it longer. Hydration can come from soup, fresh-squeezed juice, decaffeinated tea, as well as juicy fruits like watermelon. Unless you are vigilant about measuring the fluid ounces of the items listed above, you may not be able to tell if you have hydrated enough that day.

Start with a minimum of eight glasses of water per day; then, see how you feel. The amount of water someone needs really depends on several factors, but weight and activity level are significant. If you exercise often and sweat a lot, you may need more than the average person. However, if you struggle with staying on top of your hydration, these minor changes can make a big difference in your success and your vocal health. Here is a way to help determine your hydration level.

Transparent	- You are over hydrated
Lemonade	- YAY! It's just right
Light Beer	- Still good
Amber	- You are NOT hydrated
Burnt Orange	- Hydrate immediately. We will meet you at the hospital!

Sing Method

Observing Your Water

S: **Set Your Intention** - Gradually increase your water intake. Don't do it all at once. Add eight ounces a day until you feel you have met your needed water intake. For most people of average weight and height, it is at least 64 ounces of water. If you are active and sweat a lot, you will probably need to get closer to 80 or so ounces of water.

I: **Isolate From Distractions** - Throw out all the pop and sugary caffeine-laden drinks from your house. Be ruthless. Make getting a flavored latte something you do with a friend or as a reward for being more mindful. Make alcohol something you do on Friday night only.

N: **Notice Your Body** - When you feel you have a handle on your hydration, notice how much better you feel. What is your energy output? Is it different? How about your singing? Is the voice more responsive and less fatigued during and after practice? Do you have less downtime during recovery from performing or rehearsals? This awareness can inform if you are on target in your hydration effort. Listen to your body and your inner voice.

G: **Give Up Judgment** – Don't beat yourself up if you aren't able to hydrate on a busy day. Tomorrow is another day. Put a glass of water on your night stand and drink it if you wake up.

Personal Reflection

Celebrate Success: Did I consume less caffeine or slightly increase my water intake? Did I discover my water consumption is on target? Write down anything positive you observed.

Journal Kickstarters:
- Was I here today?
- Was I genuinely present?
- Did I judge myself throughout this time?
- Did I follow through on my intention?
- Did I get distracted by outside activities or the negative thoughts in my head?
- How can I be more consistent with this practice?

Additional Inquiry: What can I do to make this easier for me? Do I need to change any habits that keep me from achieving this goal?

There are some excellent water tracking apps out there. There is one that lets you grow a little plant. If you don't water it enough, it dies, and you SHOULD feel terrible. Ha! Silly little psychological thing, but it works. Try to keep that plant watered every day. I use this app; and so far, all my plants have thrived and are sitting in my virtual garden. Toni thinks this is funny! She is laughing at me as she drinks water from her fancy bottle.

Food - Don't Listen to Mary Poppins

Let food be thy medicine and medicine be thy food.

Hippocrates

We have all heard, "you are what you eat." Indeed, this is also true when talking about the voice. There are countless books, advice, and philosophies about diets for overall general health. Again, choosing what is best for you comes down to mindfulness. A diet that might be suitable for one person's general well-being might not be the same for someone else. However, there are a few basic principles that are good for all singers.

Recently, discussing "when" one eats has become almost as popular as discussing "what" one eats. Our bodies were not designed to have 24/7 access to food. Our ancient ancestors' lifestyle of feast or famine created thermogenesis, or the metabolic process by which organisms burn calories in order to generate heat. The idea of breakfast or "breaking the fast" was actually popularized during the industrial revolution. It might surprise you to learn that "breakfast is the most important meal of the day" was actually invented by a man named Harvey Kellogg. Surely there was no connection between breakfast being the most important meal of the day and his desire to sell cereal!

Flash forward to 2016, when Japanese cell biologist Yoshinori Ohsumi won the Nobel Prize in Medicine for his research on how cells recycle and renew their content through autophagy. Fasting activates autophagy, which helps slow down the aging process and has a positive impact on cell renewal. We are both fans of waiting to break our overnight fast until later in the day so we can promote autophagy.

When the body is in autophagy, it's as if Pac Man is gobbling up precancerous cells, flushing out waste, and cleaning up the entire house. There are many intermittent fasting protocols, such as:

- 12:12 – fasting overnight
- 16:8 – an eight-hour feeding window
- OMAD – one meal a day
- 5:2 – eat what you want during the week, fast on the weekend
- ADF – alternate day fasting

As with many other aspects of health, mindfulness is the key to finding what works best for your body.

Besides delaying breakfast, we enjoy practicing prolonged fasts to take advantage of the many mind, body, and spirit benefits found in this practice. Many people see the word "fasting" and think calorie restriction is bad for you, but new research shows what many cultures have been doing for a millennia, is actually beneficial. Toni enjoys quarterly fasts for three or more days, during the seasonal changes, as a reset for the body. This allows the colon to rest from processing food.

She also likes to do a fasting mimicking diet in the fall. This is a well researched and science backed protocol by Dr. Valter Longo, where the participant eats specific foods that do not signal to the brain that they have had any nourishment. In the spring she enjoys a watermelon fast. Toni buys a lot of watermelon and uses Tajin as a way to spice it up. After all she says "variety is the spice of life," and she enjoys changing it up with each season.

Hunger levels will rise and fall during a prolonged fast, but you might find your energy level and mental clarity increasing. By taking the focus off of food, one can look inward and discover new insights, which is why fasting is practiced by many faith groups. As always, consult your doctor before making any major health changes, and make sure the practice you choose will serve you well. Now let's dive into the refrigerator and discuss food.

To be clear - we are not pro-skinny. Our goal here is to help you be as healthy as you can or want to be. That being said, we are going to provide some of the latest research on nutrition and what it means for overall health. The word "diet" in this book does not mean calorie restrictions, nor does it mean eat-this-not-that; we are not endorsing any kind of fad diet. Rather, we are suggesting that you be aware of what you put in your body.

Many people suffer from food sensitivity, which can cause heartburn, mucous secretion, GERD, reflux, rashes, or hives. One should know how their body reacts to food in general. For a list of the most allergy-causing foods, check out the Food Maps Guide or mindfulnessofsinging.com for more information.

Here is the bottom line: Eating sugar, simple carbohydrates, fake fats, fake cheeses, and processed foods, is like driving yourself down a road, at a very high speed to heart disease, diabetes, cancer, and auto-immune disorders. Within the health community, this is a fact; and medical studies from all over the world confirm this fact. When the diet consists of non-processed foods, lean protein or plant-based protein; and good fats, both saturated and polyunsaturated, health will be very positively affected.

Denise understands all too well how powerful food is for health. Here is her story: I have pretty good genes. My mom is currently 96. She is pretty sharp mentally but has joint pain and bad knees. She is so mentally sharp that sometimes I wish she would forget some stuff. However, my dad recently passed. He was 96 years old, and he and my mom would have celebrated 78 years of marriage three weeks after he passed. Before his death, he could run around the block, but may not remember how to get home. Together they were a whole person. My mom was determined for them to live and die in their own house rather than go to an assisted living facility. They could do that until my dad's dementia became too difficult for her to manage. They were 96 when they finally moved to an assisted living facility. My dad would have lived longer, but they both got COVID-19. My mom was fine, but my dad's illness had a huge impact on him neurologically. It pushed him into the final stages of dementia. My maternal grandparents lived neither long nor happy lives. My grandpa died in the cornfield of a massive coronary at age 60. His wife lived another 15 years but was wracked with arthritis; and frankly, a bad attitude. She was the most unhappy person I ever knew. I didn't understand this as a child; but as an adult, I learned of her terrible and traumatic childhood. It is no wonder she was depressed, unhappy, and overcome with physical pain.

My paternal grandparents lived long, but again, not happy lives. Around the age of 70, my grandpa began getting lost on his farm, unable to remember how to get home. By age 75, he was in an elder care facility. It was awful. He didn't know where he was and didn't recognize his wife when she entered the room.

His life with dementia is something I am determined not to experience. My father's dementia came later, but it is still an indicator that something in their diet triggered an expression of a gene that causes vascular dementia. Their diet consisted of refined sugar, a lot of lard, processed flour; fried foods all cooked in aluminum pans, and they drank their well water out of an aluminum bucket. Research shows that sugar is the leading cause of vascular decline. There is no white sugar in my house, and there hasn't been since my last child was born in 1998.

When my youngest son was born, I also had an 18-month-old baby. (Don't ask. Surprise!) I was 60 pounds overweight, not singing, and I felt terrible. I had swelling in my joints, and the fat on my body meant that I had inflammation everywhere. I was not eating well, was stressed, and tired. I went to the doctor because my hands were killing me, and my knuckles looked distorted. She took a blood test and told me I had markers for lupus and rheumatoid arthritis (RA). She wanted to do more blood tests. I asked her if steroids were the only treatment possible if the test for lupus was positive. "Yes," was her reply. I promptly left her office and went on a quest to find out if my diet could reverse my symptoms.

This led me to several studies that linked sugar and processed foods to RA and other auto-immune diseases. So, for Lent that year

I gave up sugar. I didn't eat a single piece of chocolate! Wow! To know me is to buy me chocolate. My diet at the time consisted of what I thought was healthy for me based on the "food pyramid." What a joke! For breakfast, I had granola and skim milk. Lunch was a sandwich with lean meat or a bagel with low-fat cream cheese. I always had a diet Coke. To round out my day, I made pasta or a rice dish and a salad. No wonder I was in terrible health. All of those refined carbs and fake foods made my body sick! When I cut out the sugar and processed foods for those six weeks of Lent, I lost my baby weight, and all the swelling in my hands disappeared. I also got back to singing, in part because I wasn't tired, and my voice felt terrific.

After making those dietary changes, I had my blood work tested; and it showed no markers for arthritis of any kind! Earlier, I mentioned my sister died of cancer. My sister's diet was trash. There was diet Coke in the fridge at all times, potato chips, pasta, refined cereals, and white bread. When she made pasta sauce, she put in half a cup of sugar. She loved to bake cookies and cakes. When she got sick, she got rid of sugar and flour in her kitchen; but honestly, it was too late. I can't stress it enough: food can either slowly kill you, or it can be medicine. Toni and I strongly believe in the Ayurvedic proverb: "When the diet is wrong, medicine is of no use; When the diet is right, medicine is of no need."

Read studies and books on longevity, cancer research, and auto-immune disease prevention, and you will learn many of the same things. If you want to stay on this earth for a decent amount of time, while feeling good and remaining intact mentally, food is key. Research in this area is growing rapidly as the mysteries of our

DNA and the genome are uncovered. Arm yourself with knowledge, so you can live a long vital life!

Recognizing potential saboteurs both in the kitchen and our personal lives is also a game-changer in our effort to be healthier. Sometimes when we're trying to do something healthful, whether it is exercising, losing five pounds, or hydrating more; people become weird. Suddenly you're in a toxic environment. I have an acquaintance who is always asking me what I am doing for my health; and when I tell her, she replies "Well, I heard that's not good for you." I fall for it every time. Another example, maybe your significant other says, "Ooh come on, you know I like meat on your bones." I have a friend who lost 100 pounds, and her husband bought her a size XXXL blouse for her birthday and said, "You know, just in case." Realizing that some folks may see progress in others as a personal affront to them, enables us to be better equipped to deal with them.

Since food is one of the more difficult things to tackle, we want to give you a few things to consider before you begin your practice.

- First set achievable goals.
- Don't try to eat the whole enchilada all at once.
- Overcoming ingrained poor health habits can be an overwhelming task for many individuals.
- Avoid discussing efforts to change diet with friends or family who may have negative input.
- Go back and look at your questionnaire.

Which question needs the most attention? Which is less dire? Aristotle said, "Knowing yourself is the beginning of all wisdom." If you know that doing the hardest thing first will be easier for you; and it is in your personality to conquer the hard stuff early, start there. If small steps and easily achievable goals are a turn on for you, do them first. Perhaps, addressing one harmful habit daily is the preferred choice. The important thing is to establish a pattern that will lead to success. Once successful with a particular goal, other issues can be addressed as well.

Sing Method

Noticing Your Food

***S*: Set Your Intention** - Choose an unhealthy food and eliminate it from your diet. Then, trade it for a healthier choice. Perhaps you like chips, (Denise's weakness - "Prime Rib and Horseradish potato chips" are her favorite!) trade those out for kale chips (Toni's favorite) or a gluten-free organic cracker.

***I*: Isolate From Distractions** - Once you have chosen which food you will eliminate, you can address the distractions. Throw away unhealthy foods and give yourself some positive reinforcement. Choose a small reward for your sacrifice. If you are worried about wasting food, take the non-perishable items to the food bank. Give the rest of the unopened food to a friend down the street who can afford to eat or who has great self-control. Ha! That will teach them! Oops...our mindfulness is slipping here.

***N*: Notice Your Body** - How does your body feel when you eat foods that are good for you? If you are trying to pinpoint food sensitivities, see if you sing better after eliminating what once caused body inflammation. Did something you eat cause extra phlegm or dry out your vocal cords? Or after eating your favorite pasta dish, did you experience fatigue? Isn't it a relief to know that when you eat something that your body rejects, it isn't just because of age, or it's just in your head, you really can feel great after you have eaten well.

G: **Give Up Judgment** – Did I just eat ALL of that? Guilt after eating, Ugh! We have all been there. If you enjoyed a piece of birthday cake, just sing happy birthday, really loudly! Let it go! The point of this exercise is to notice the times bad choices were made and remember how you felt afterward. Recognize the things that distract you from mindful practice. Keep at it; stay focused. Close your eyes and sing. Those thoughts of guilt, shame, and self-loathing will pass.

Personal Reflection

Celebrate Success: Did giving up one unhealthy food motivate me to give up other unhealthy foods? Did I feel better when I changed my eating habits?

Journal Kickstarters:
- Was I here today?
- Was I genuinely present?
- Did I judge myself throughout this time?
- Did I follow through on my intention?
- Did I get distracted by outside activity or negative thoughts in my head?

Additional Inquiry: Are any of my food choices associated with comforting myself? What other choices can I make? Would I benefit from having an accountability buddy?

Exercise - Move That Body

Because of the negativity associated with the word "exercise," we want to help you create a "dynamic movement" practice that will have you looking forward to the opportunity of moving your body in a way that will nourish your mind, body, and spirit. What do you need specifically in terms of a dynamic movement practice? The best dynamic movement practice — wait for it — is the one you will actually do! Toni needs lots of variety. Doing the same physical activity every day, no matter how terrific the program might be, will create boredom for her. If that resonates with you, there are endless opportunities to move your body. Don't guilt-trip yourself into believing only one particular type of movement is the gospel. On the flip side, if you need consistency, find something that works well for you and enjoy yourself.

At the beginning of the book, we presented a series of questions to help you plan your most productive singing practice. We have included those same questions here to enable you to discover a dynamic movement practice to enhance mindfulness of the whole body, which is your instrument.

Why - First, know "why" you want to create a movement practice. Sometimes it is extremely helpful to review all the benefits you will receive for investing this time in yourself. Probably, you are already well aware of the many benefits of exercise. However, there may be some additional benefits that are new to you. Recent research has shown that a sedentary lifestyle is equal to smoking a pack of cigarettes per day. Studies also suggest that to have a healthy cardiovascular system, 20 to 30 minutes of brisk walking or somewhere around 7,000 to 10,000 steps a day is adequate. Tracking apps, watches and rings are beneficial for this. Also, standing 12 times over twelve hours is a good start for giving yourself a break from the office cubicle, classroom chairs, or couch. If it seems overwhelming at first or if you are like Denise and HATE exercise, start with small steps or find a movement practice that brings you joy or peace. Exercise can also deliver some impactful results in the spirit realm as well.

The key is addressing the benefit that is most appealing to you. Do you need to move more in order to sleep better at night? Would you like to have more energy during the day? Do you desire to eliminate some of your current medications? Maybe you and your partner would love to increase your libido, or would you love to simply get high on a dopamine rush? Adding a movement practice will certainly benefit your overall level of mindfulness and your respiratory health which will directly benefit your voice.

The benefit that made Denise decide exercising wasn't so bad is the research about exercise and the brain. Who wants an increased risk for Alzheimer's? Research has proven for several years that physical activity protects the brain from some effects of aging. In some of those studies, animals that exercised gained more new neurons and a better memory than their sedentary counterparts. Other similar studies have shown that older people who increased their daily steps added volume in portions of their brains associated with memory. Even subjects who were young and more fit than their peers performed better on cognitive tests.

However, there are still some mysteries, associated with how, at a cellular level, exercise alters the brain and its function. Researchers presume the process involves the release of chemicals in the brain and throughout the body when one exercises. These chemicals cause a chain reaction that ultimately alters how the brain functions. What isn't clear is what these chemicals are and from where they originate. Scientists are making new discoveries every day about the brain and its many mysteries. It is an exciting time to be a neuroscientist. Isn't science cool?

When - Discover the optimal time for you to move your body. Following our body's circadian rhythms is a large component of the ancient practices of Ayurveda (ai-yr-VAY·duh), which literally means "the science of life." By adhering to our natural cycles and rhythms, we can help our bodies' ability to detoxify and achieve greater health and wellbeing. Thus, Ayurvedic practices can provide a model for which activities correlate best with our circadian rhythms. If you have struggled with finding the right time for your movement practice, perhaps it would be helpful to discover your circadian rhythm and see if you can adjust your schedule to promote harmony within your natural body clock.

Most individuals, regardless of their circadian rhythm, will have a better night's sleep if they avoid exercise too late in the evening. If you are an early bird, an early morning workout can be absolutely exhilarating, although your night owl friends might beg to differ. Give yourself the best opportunity to be successful by determining the best time for you to move that body!

Where - One of the first steps in creating a successful movement practice is to put yourself in a space that you really enjoy. If you hate the environment of a gym, chances are no matter how great the equipment is, you will have a hard time motivating yourself to go. If you love being outdoors, choose a movement practice that will give you the opportunity to soak up some sunshine and move at the same time.

By the way, new research indicates that all of our avoidance of the sun is a mistake. We need the healing properties it provides. Also, there is evidence to suggest that if your nutritional needs are in good balance you will sunburn less. Toni and I are fair-skinned, and we can both attest to the fact that we get less sunburn now than we did ten years ago, even though neither of us uses sunscreen because of the chemicals the manufacturers put in them.

If being outdoors doesn't excite or interest you, find the best match for yourself indoors. We all know what we really like, don't put yourself in a space that you won't really enjoy. If the people in that exercise class are bringing you down, then look for a different tribe. To ensure your success, be certain your BPT (Biological Peak Time) and your surroundings will work well together.

Toni loves to exercise outdoors and frequently stands on her head in the middle of the field. Even though her neighbors may think she's lost it, it makes her happy. I, on the other hand, like a spa feeling; and even though traditional gyms turn me off, I will go to one if there is a relaxing reward at the end. Consequently, I chose a gym that has a massage bed; and when I am done with 20 minutes of cardio and weightlifting, I RUN to that bed. I can't wait to go to the gym because of that one little perk.

What - "What" is not as important as DO IT! Just move. If you are a fairly sedentary person your challenge is to walk 10,000 steps.

Get outside or go to the mall or gym. If you have the opportunity to walk outside, take your shoes off and enjoy the many benefits of grounding. Where doesn't matter, just move. Be creative with your movement practice. Enjoy something new. When was the last time you took a nature walk or went to a botanical garden? Mindfulness is about listening to that inner voice and letting the child in you come out and play. Park the car in the back of the parking lot; think of it as a generous act, and let others have that spot right by the door. Take the stairs. A friend suddenly seemed thinner; and when asked how she did it, she replied "I quit taking the elevator."

Starting small makes an enormous impact. Do what we call "automatic" habits. Try to incorporate small habits throughout the day that will have a significant impact. Find one habit that is already part of your day and pair it with another. For instance, try doing squats while you brush your teeth. If you have a toothbrush that vibrates for two minutes, start doing squats when you begin and don't stop until the brush has finished its two-minute pattern. This will give you a new automatic habit. Sometimes Denise does an exercise in the kitchen when she is waiting for something to cook or boil. Not only does this pass the time, but also increases her steps or movement for the day.

Remember, we are NOT advocating getting thinner; we are advocating getting healthier!

Obviously, as a yoga teacher, Toni has a bias toward yoga as an excellent movement practice. Yoga is a wonderful match for singers, as the ability to bring awareness to one's breath is vitally important in singing. Singing also requires the duality of strength and relaxation found in yoga practice. In Sanskrit yoga literally means "to join" or "to yoke" together.

Many people see yoga as simply doing crazy "asanas" or postures; however, the real beauty of the practice is the yoking together of breathwork and meditation through the poses. Yoga also helps calm and center the mind, as well as improving one's feeling of well-being. In addition to the body and spirit benefits, Harvard Health Publishing states that yoga "actually makes your brain work better." In fact, studies have shown that people who regularly do yoga have a thicker cerebral cortex and hippocampus. Both of these areas of the brain are responsible for information processing, learning, memory, and language. That's enough to make anyone want to do headstands or twist like a pretzel. Although, you certainly don't have to start there! To get started, take a beginner class or explore the wide variety of different yoga practices. It truly is a great way to harmonize mind, body, and spirit, and a perfect movement practice for singers!

Below is a list of creative exercise movements that can be easily incorporated into daily routines.

- Pace when talking on the phone
- Rent a canoe, kayak, SUP board, etc.
- Play hide and seek with the kids - They will think you are a superhero!
- Take a moonlight stroll with a loved one
- Put your laundry in a big basket and do curls with it 20 times

- Do curls 10 times each arm when taking the milk jug out of the fridge
- Do partner yoga
- Put on 80's music and dance like it's 1999
- Ride a bike
- Play pickleball, tennis, racket ball
- Play golf

You get the idea. Your workout can be as creative as your imagination. Listen to your inner voice. What makes a movement practice unsustainable is telling yourself that you need to do something that you absolutely detest. Ask the question; "When was there a time that I moved my body and enjoyed it?" Do that!

Sing Method

Finding a Movement Practice

***S*: Set Your Intention** - Make it a goal to choose a dynamic movement practice today. If you are already moving daily, choose what you hear your inner voice nudging you to do. Your subconscious wants you to live and be well. When you walk by that Stairmaster, and your little voice says, "I'm going to do that someday," Listen! That's a sign that your subconscious is trying to tell you to move more and become even more healthy. Make today that day. We said to do what you love. However, if you absolutely hate the Stairmaster (like we do), do something that is more enjoyable for you. The subconscious doesn't care what it is specifically; it just wants you to get your blood moving, feeding your brain and body with those anti-aging chemicals.

***I*: Isolate From Distractions** - As mentioned before, sometimes the distraction is simply avoidance. Enlist the help of a friend by having an accountability partner. It's harder to put off your movement practice if you know your friend is outside waiting for you. If you need further incentive, get a book on Audible or listen to our podcast as you do your daily movement practice.

When Toni and I were working on our masters' degrees, we joined with several of our classmates and made a pact. We went to aerobics together, and whoever missed had to put money in the jar.

At the end of the month, we used that money to go to lunch. It was a win-win. At least until the instructor kicked us out because we wouldn't stop talking. Loquacious singers - whatcha gonna do?

N: **Notice Your Body** - Sore? Tired? Energized? Sleeping better? Singing better? All of these things are probably showing up. Concentrate on the good things you feel. Your muscles will adapt to the new demands. Drinking more water will help ease the soreness and so will a beautiful magnesium bath. You can even try Cryotherapy or cold therapy. A cryotherapy chamber is a tank that will get down to around minus 300 degrees Fahrenheit; you stand in it for up to three minutes. Other options include taking a cold shower or bath, sitting in a tub of ice water, or going outside in the winter without a coat for about 10 minutes, if it isn't below zero. Just be sure you protect those fingers and toes.

G: **Give Up Judgment** – Feel fat? Feet too tired to do it today? Don't let that little voice inside convince you that you have to be skinny to get out and do your movement practice, or that you're always too tired, and this just won't work for you. That is "self-sabotage" talking, and they are a jerk. Slap them down and stay positive! Don't listen to them.

Personal Reflection

Celebrate Success: What did I enjoy the most about my new movement practice? Did I experience an increase in energy? Finding a movement activity you can enjoy will keep you coming back for more!

Journal Kickstarters:
- Was I here today?
- Was I genuinely present?
- Did I judge myself throughout this time?
- Did I follow through on my intention?
- Did I get distracted by outside activities or the negative thoughts in my head?
- How can I be more consistent with this practice?

Additional Inquiry: If this was challenging, what would make it easier? Is this an activity that I would also benefit from having an accountability buddy? What is holding me back?

Sleep - Restore Your Voice

Sleep is sometimes the overlooked health habit for proper singing. We think of sleep as a time when the body and the brain shut down, but it is much more than that. Sleep is an active part of what our body does for recovery. We do a lot of memory consolidation and brain strengthening when we sleep. Toni and I both use sleep tracking devices. Toni uses a Fitbit, and I use an Oura ring. Both track our deep, light, and REM sleep, as well as our heart rate variability. They have been a great tool for us, as we can tweak our sleep needs based on the data we get from the apps. We take in vast amounts of information throughout our day. Rather than recording them in real-time, our brain stores the information; and it gets processed when we sleep. Think of it as a computer update. This is why, when learning something such as a language or a new skill, sleep is vital to the retention of the new habit or talent.

Singers take in millions of visual and sound cues while memorizing and singing pages of music. If they aren't sleeping, they may struggle to achieve their goals. The brain is adapting, sending messages in milliseconds to muscles of the larynx, ribcage, diaphragm, and so on. Really, we could go on and on. You get it, right? Consequently, it's really important for not only singers but everyone to get sufficient sleep! Lack of sleep not only causes the brain and the body to function less optimally, but when sleep-deprived, the voice does not work. Phonation is challenging at best and hard to manage. Not to mention (except we are) mental fatigue is also a significant consequence of sleep deprivation.

Research shows that after sleep, people retain information and perform better on tests. The body also needs sleep for the restoration of muscle and tissue repair, and to make and produce much-needed hormones. We have seen many students try to perform after not sleeping properly, and the results have not been positive! When a person sings, the neurotransmitters involved are numerous. The singer is multi-tasking, and the brain is overloaded. Singers need to be concerned with body awareness; as well knowing and remembering the words, the rhythms, and the pitches. After trying to learn the melody of a song, if the body doesn't get the required rest, learning lyrics is much harder.

Sound sleep is crucial for everyone at every age. No matter how old you are, everyone needs to retain information and learn skills for life. It is a myth that you can make up for lost sleep; there is no such thing. The best sleep hygiene is a consistent sleep routine.

Bright lights and screens have a way of keeping us from getting the best sleep we can, so turn off any bright lights a couple of hours before going to bed. We suggest buying a pair of blue light blocking glasses if it's necessary to stay on the phone or computer. Toni wears Dave Asprey's glasses. I bought a pair from my eye doctor.

Napping during the day is not a good idea. This can also disrupt the sleep cycle. Turn down the temperature in the bedroom. It is a known fact that a cool room makes for better sleep. Also, limit caffeine intake during the day. This can wreak havoc on sleep. I have nothing with caffeine in it past 3:00 p.m., not even dark chocolate! Gasp! I know, right? Toni never has caffeine because it wires her all day, affects her sleep, and dehydrates her. Love your coffee or the taste of coffee? Try Teeccino, it is an herbal coffee that provides energy without the stimulants. Another healthy way to wean from drinking too much coffee is to switch to Dandy Blend. This herbal beverage made from dandelions has zero caffeine, no acidity, no bitterness; and for many people, it works as a substitute for coffee.

Finally, don't let stress get the best of you. If you feel stressed, make a to-do list for tomorrow, and then forget about it tonight. Try to meditate before you go to bed. Do some breathwork. Take a bath in a candlelit room and breathe slowly and deeply. Have a bedtime habit and stick to it. Along with water intake, I programmed my bedtime on my phone through an app. (Toni doesn't need this as she falls over dead asleep by 9:30). At 9:15 PM my Oura Smart Ring reminds me it is getting close to my optimal bedtime. Your usual routine might be to wash your face, brush your teeth and take a relaxing bath or shower. Choose whatever will help your mind and body know that sleep is coming. Tracking your sleep can be a useful way of distinguishing if tiredness is because of a habit or a health problem. Being armed with information is often the key to finding better health. Mouth taping, discussed under breathwork, is also a method of signaling the body that sleep is on the way.

One final tip: perhaps you have great sleep hygiene habits, yet wake up during the night. This can certainly put a damper on those cumulative hours of deep sleep. Don't panic! If you wake up, one of the best things you can do is NOT look at the clock. Every time you awaken, and look at the clock, you are programming your body to remember waking up again at that time. Taking a few slow light breaths and relaxing will often get you back to dreamland much faster than observing the time and thinking negative thoughts, such as "Holy cow it can't be 3:00 a.m! What am I doing awake? I will never feel rested for that meeting today!" Calmly changing your sleep position and pondering what you were dreaming can get you back to snoozing again much more quickly. If you need to get up and go to the bathroom during the night, try to use minimal lighting in order to keep your mind and body in the sleep space.

If you try Denise's Sleepy Time Gelatine, you probably won't even need to worry about looking at the clock, as you will be sleeping through the night! If you are interested in the gelatine, the recipe is below. If you don't like jello, you can make it without the gelatine; and boom, you have a mocktail.

SLEEPYTIME JELLO

Ingredients

- 1 Packet Knox gelatin powder (1/4 ounce)
- 1 Cup 100% fruit juice
- 1 Cup Valerian Tea (follow box instructions)
- 1 or 2 Tablespoons Glycine (to taste)
- 8 Tablespoons of Magnesium Powder (I like *Doctor's Best*)

DIRECTIONS:
Soften gelatine in 1/2 cup of the juice.

Put remaining juice into a small saucepan with glycine and Valerian Tea and bring to a boil.

Remove from heat and add softened gelatine, stirring until dissolved.

Add magnesium powder, and pour into mold or dish.

Refrigerate until firm, about 3 hours.

Top with Coco Whip (No cool whip!!)

Serves four - but you only need to eat half of a serving.

Sing Method

Tracking Your Sleep

S: **Set Your Intention** - Find a sleep tracking app, and use it if you are not sure about your sleep quality. If you are waking up feeling tired after seven hours of sleep or more, see a doctor. Be honest with yourself here. Are you tired? Do you take little naps? If so, add an hour and see if it helps. How many hours of sleep do you think you need? Find out, don't guess. Make your next couple of weeks about determining how much sleep is best for you. Toni needs seven hours; I need at least eight.

I: **Isolate From Distractions** - As stated above, develop a ritual. Some medical professionals say to start your routine two to three hours before bed. Put your phone, computer, iPad, and all other screens away at least two hours before bed. Additionally, remove food and drink items that keep you from sleeping well. Ask yourself: Is it worth it? If so, allow yourself those fun moments. If not, try to remember to make a mental note of how badly you will feel and choose to stick to your intention next time.

N: **Notice Your Body** - How does your body feel when you sing? If you aren't sleeping well, you will probably notice the voice is a little rough or husky. How about the throat itself? How does it feel when you are well-rested? The difference should be striking.

G: **Give Up Judgment** – If you still aren't sleeping well, don't judge yourself too harshly. There is a reason. There are sleep clinics all over the world. Seek the advice of a medical professional and make sure there isn't another underlying cause for poor sleep. You may have been doing everything within your control.

Personal Reflection

Celebrate Success: If you shut your phone off earlier at night, used blue light blocking glasses, or made any small changes write it down! Our sleep hygiene habits are often deeply ingrained routines. Waking up rested will make you realize the change was well worth the reward.

Journaling Kickstarters:
- Was I here today?
- Was I genuinely present?
- Did I judge myself throughout this time?
- Did I follow through on my intention?
- Did I get distracted by outside activity or the negative thoughts in my head?

Additional Inquiry: What is holding me back from making the changes I need to make? Is it time to seek professional help from a sleep clinic? This is our last SING Method for Body as the Instrument. What do you need to change to give your instrument a tune-up?

Chapter Six

Take Center Stage

Creating the Final Harmony

Since you have been harmonizing your mind, body, and spirit, it's time to put the rubber to the road and sing for a real person! We realize asking you to sing for someone might actually create fear and distractions. In the previous chapters, we have encouraged you to isolate yourself from distractions. In this, our last chapter, we invite you to embrace the distractions like Denise embraced her pain. We have saved the hardest challenge for the last.

Tiger Woods, one of the greatest golf players of all time, began his training with his father. When Tiger was very young, his father would intentionally try to break his focus by jeering at him while on the golf course. His father knew that down the road, no matter how much Tiger prepared, there would always be distractions on the course. People are supposed to be quiet during a golf tournament; but often people talk, whisper, cough, sneeze, etc., which could be very distracting to the golfer.

By singing in front of others you may find that you are experiencing some mental distractions. Now is the time to eliminate those distracting thoughts and emotional responses, and create your own protocol to find a place of quiet and peace as you sing. Use your favorite meditation tools to help you be brave, bold, and vulnerable enough to share your spirit with someone by singing for them.

We never know what might happen during a performance. A phone might go off, or someone might sneeze during your high note. Sometimes occurrences can be even more extreme. During one of Toni's performances, someone actually died! She had to keep singing. Someone fainted behind Denise in the choir and took out the percussion section, making quite a helluva racket. The show had to go on. To sing through distraction is definitely a challenge and a significant struggle for Denise. She confesses that when someone in the audience picks their nose or a baby cries, she can easily get distracted. Remember baby Jesus? She is continually working on this.

Training for inevitable distractions can help us stay in a spiritual place rather than the earthly one that would keep us from having an authentic experience. We have some great ideas in this SING Method to help prepare for potential distractions. Those who really want to get to a new level of courage, send us an email with a sample of you singing. We would love to hear from you! Email us at mindfulnessofsinging@gmail.com.

Sing Method

Singing For Someone

***S*: Set Your Intention** - Congrats on making it to graduation day! Armed with a new level of mindfulness, it's time to sing for someone and embrace distractions.

***I*: Isolate From Distractions** - Now is the time to work within the boundless possibilities of distraction. Distractions are inevitable. Like it or not; life, as well as performing for others, is full of distractions. The assignment is to ask someone to make faces or gestures while you sing. Try to stay in the moment, even if it becomes very difficult. Don't get tickled, although we imagine this will be funny, which is useful because we should never take ourselves too seriously. The key to this exercise is knowing yourself. While we want to challenge you with the concept of actually working with distractions; some of you may find the experience of singing for someone high on the distraction scale. If that's you, give yourself a break; and sing the song through once without added distractions.

***N*: Notice Your Body** - When your friend observed your singing, how did your body respond? Did it betray you? Were you consumed with fear or worry? Ask yourself, not your mind, but deep within your spirit, what were you feeling? If you noticed an elevated heart rate or fast breathing, were you associating it with excitement; or was the fight or flight instinct kicking in?

That flight or fight reaction is an indication that you were afraid. Even more importantly, were you able to sing anyway and stay in the moment? Did you choose a reaction, or did the response choose you?

G: **Give Up Judgment** – First, if you did the "intention" of this chapter, by singing for someone, give yourself a fist bump! That's right; put two hands up to the roof, pump them a couple of times and say, "I am awesome. I did it!" Because you were fearless (or at least trying to be anyway)! If you were still really distracted and couldn't stay in the moment, keep working towards a more present experience. Do the exercise again, maybe with someone less funny.

Personal Reflection

Celebrate Success: Did I rise to the challenge of embracing distractions and singing for someone? If you can sing for one person, you can probably sing for many more. Sometimes, it's more intimidating to sing for someone you know in an intimate setting than to sing for an entire audience. Congrats! When is your next gig?

Journaling Kickstarters:
- Was I here today?
- Was I genuinely present?
- Did I judge myself throughout this time?
- Did I follow through on my intention?
- Did I get distracted by outside activity or the negative thoughts in my head?

Additional Inquiry: Would I enjoy singing for more people? How could I make the experience more enjoyable? Did I use all the tools I have learned throughout the book? What songs would I want to sing? You certainly don't have to perform to reap all the benefits from the mindfulness of singing, but it doesn't hurt to journal, daydream, and see what your heart desires.

Final questions: What is the greatest challenge I have overcome in this journey? What is the driftwood that I haven't let go of yet? Complete this sentence: Next year, more than anything, I hope my singing...

Before Enlightenment: Chop Wood, Carry Water.
After Enlightenment: Chop Wood, Carry Water.

A Zen Proverb

Closing

Imagine you have just been given a Stradivarius violin! They are worth millions of dollars, hailed as one of the best instruments; and they are extremely rare (only 650 are still available). They were made in the 1700s by famous violin maker, Antonio Stradivari.

Imagine being given this violin, tossing it in the trunk of your car or throwing it in between your kid's field hockey sticks, a stack of books, and an opened bag of potting soil. A person would have to be crazy to do that! Even while you are reading this you may be thinking "This is absurd; what's the point?"

The point is, absolutely no other instrument is as intrinsically tied to the individual as the voice. Every other instrument is played upon. We beat the drums, strum the guitar, play the piano, etc.; but when we sing, we literally are playing upon ourselves and our very soul. Think about how much you would take care of that precious violin; you would go to all kinds of measures to make certain it would remain playable. In part, because if it couldn't be played, it would become worthless. All those millions of dollars were for nothing. Think about how much more vulnerable and valuable our bodies and tiny vocal cords are. Our vocal cords are less than an inch long and housed inside an intricate body constantly performing millions of functions all day long. What a gift, how precious is this ability to communicate with our voice not only in speech but in music and song!

We so often see people who want to sing, but misuse their bodies, talents, and dreams as if they are going to be able to replace them if they are abused or lost. This is why we are encouraging you to be present, aware, and actively caring for the precious gifts you have been given: the desire and the ability to sing!

All the tools learned in the *Mindfulness of Singing* can help preserve your own Stradivarius voice; a voice that can help you communicate with others, sing to a child, or soothe yourself. These tools can create real, sustainable personal growth when applied to daily habits and lifestyle.

*May your chopping of wood and carrying of water,
be blessed with an abundance of song!*

Toni Crowder

In closing let's review all the tools at your disposal. Using the four key steps of the SING Method helps with initinating change:

Set Your Intention

Isolate From Distractions

Notice Your Body

Give Up Judgment

What if you read and meditated upon the *Singers Meditation and Affirmation* every day? How would those positive, self-affirming statements affect your life?

Have you stepped back recently to unpack your own Plan for Success?

The Plan for Success outline is:

Why - What is your motivation and reason for singing or anything else that occupies your time?

When - Are you singing? Are you playing? When are you actually doing the things you love?

Declutter - Are there physical things, toxic people, or other things that you need to address in your life?

Lighting - What's the environment like where you sing and where you spend your time?

What - Are you actually singing things you love? Are you feeding your soul?

How - How are you doing with exploring singing? Has it become the dreaded practice or a time for play?

How is journaling working for you? Perhaps, go back and apply those many journaling questions and prompts to other areas of your life; make them fit your own situation. Have you reviewed previous entries? Seeing them again with fresh eyes might help you discover a nugget of gold that you missed.

Perhaps the most difficult thing in life is to manage your own thoughts and mind. How is your Battle for the Mind going? We get it! It is an ongoing daily battle; we must make the choice to face our own issues. Have you been less judgmental with yourself, with others? Has your journey uncovered any traumas that need to be faced and addressed? We encourage you to continue your work by confronting the things that stand in your way. If you have been struggling with some issues for a long time, we encourage you to be courageous, bold, and, when necessary, ask for help. Think of seeing a mental health professional as an investment in yourself and a beautiful way to honor your future self.

Remember the Longfellow quote, "The Voice is the Organ of the Soul." Are you facing your singing and life's journey with fear or love? After all, The Spirit Sets the Tone. What motivates you? Is the spirit you bring to singing and life in alignment with your vision for yourself? Are you finding breathwork practice or meditation more helpful? Perhaps a combination of both are serving you best. If a practice becomes stale, go back and review all the many options for seeking meditation and mindfulness found in Chapter Four. We hope the ideas presented to you will inspire a hunger for more knowledge and experiences that will bring peace and zen to your overall life.

Has the information in Body is the Instrument, given you any new thoughts about your water intake, food, exercise, or sleep? Did one particular area jump out as a topic that needs more attention? We know intuitively what we need to change. Sometimes it's just a matter of setting up enough friction or interference to stop a bad habit. Conversely, setting up positive baby steps to get us started on the things we need to address is also a great way to make those difficult changes in lifestyle. If you mastered one area, good for you! Use that momentum to build upon another success.

It has been said that Mariah Carey insured her voice for $35 million dollars and that according to the UK's Daily Mail, Queen frontman Adam Lambert's voice is insured for $54 million? We truly believe the things mentioned above will keep you covered! The tools we've offered can help ensure that your voice stays healthy and serves you well; not only as long as you want to sing, but as long as you live.

Finally, wherever you are in your journey; there is no shame or judgment, just the chance to pick yourself up, dust yourself off, and start all over again. Believe in yourself and the Stradivarius that you hold inside of you!

Here's to many more lovely songs. There will be days you don't feel like singing, but we hope you will Sing Anyway!

Sing Anyway

by Toni Crowder

Sometimes I just don't feel like singing.

Sing anyway, and most likely your mood will change.

Sometimes I don't think my voice is pretty enough.

Sing anyway, your authentic, honest voice *is* pretty.

Sometimes I just don't have enough time to sing.

Sing anyway, sing in your car, sing in the shower,

sing on your walk.

Sometimes I think I am too old to sing.

Sing anyway, you are never too old, too young,

too fat, too thin, too rich or too broke to SING!

About the Authors

Dr. Denise Ritter Bernardini has taught Voice and Opera at the University level for over 20 years. She has taught at Radford University, Oklahoma City University, University of Oklahoma, Indiana Purdue University, Manchester University, University of Toledo, and Grace College. She has performed internationally and throughout the US with Orchestra and Symphonic Organizations as well as Opera Festivals and Companies. Denise has been a soloist in prestigious venues, such as Carnegie Hall, and a recitalist in London, England; Tbilisi, Republic of Georgia; and at the Certosa di Garegnano in Milan, Italy. She has also performed her one-woman classical cabaret in Leibniz, Austria, where she performed for the International University Global Theater to an audience representing 32 countries.

Dr. Bernardini has completed over 40 graduate hours in mental health with an emphasis on mindfulness and performance anxiety pathologies. She is a presenter on the mindfulness of singing for educators and singers. The Governor's School of the Commonwealth of Virginia named Dr. Bernardini the Director of

Vocal Studies in 2023. This is the largest fine arts program sponsored by the Department of Education in Virginia.

Denise leads a support group for music students to explore performance anxiety issues, and to develop resilience/coping mechanisms for performance success. She has written for the *Journal of Singing* about mental health in the applied vocal studio. Her quantitative and qualitative study, *The Healthy Voice Protocol*, concentrated on food as medicine, and movement to give resilience and increase stamina, for the aging singer.

An avid social justice advocate, Denise is currently involved in a project focused on bringing awareness to human trafficking. *A Thousand Hands: A Million Stars* is an all-female artist collaboration which includes poetry, music, dance, and art. This unique one-of-a-kind performance has been presented at the annual Conference for Human Trafficking in Toledo, Ohio, at the city's premier arts showcase, Momentum; Ohio University in Athens, Ohio; Chapman University in Orange, California; Santa Clara University in Santa Clara, California; and Reinhardt University in Waleska, Georgia.

Dr. Bernardini is also a sought-after clinician, teacher, presenter, and author. She has presented at The Voice Symposium in Philadelphia, Pennsylvania; the International Congress of Voice Teachers in Stockholm, Sweden; the Great Lakes Regional Conference of College Music Society; the Indiana Music Educators Convention; and several National Association of Teachers of Singing regional and state-level clinics.

Denise's book *A Stylistic Guide of Classical Cabaret: A Stylistic and Historical Glimpse with selected songs by Satie, Poulenc, Schönberg, Weill, Britten, and Moore* can be purchased through Amazon.

ABOUT THE AUTHORS

Toni Crowder taught on the voice faculty at Randolph-Macon College and has been a guest clinician at schools across the state of Virginia. Her background and training as a Music Educator, Music Therapist, CYVT (certified YogaVoice® practitioner) and RYT-200 (Yoga Alliance Registered 200-hour yoga teacher) helped her create an award-winning vocal studo. Recently, as a result of her own mindfulness of singing journey, Toni has been creating original compositions, singing light jazz, and accompanying herself on the piano for live music venues.

Ms. Crowder's most notable role is her original one-woman show as the bright-nosed, goofy-stockinged, song-slinging Opera Clown Tessitura. With Young Audiences of Virginia, The Virginia National Federation of Music Club, Opera Roanoke, and the Fairfax Arts Council Creative Arts Roster, she entertained thousands of children and adults at schools, libraries, museums, and festivals across the state of Virginia. Highlights from her tours include performing for the Todi Music Festival Portsmouth, (sister program to Todi Italy) Classical Singer international singer convention in New York, and tours throughout Washington D. C., New Jersey, New Mexico, Texas, Maryland, New Hampshire, and Arkansas.

She has also entertained audiences without her clown nose and Viking horns! The *Washington Post* hailed her performance of Rosalinda in *Die Fledermaus* as being "full of vigor and excitement." She carried that same energy into televised and radio recordings of her performance of Mendelssohn duets with international soprano Lucy Shelton for National Public Radio's *Performance Today* and Backstage Pass's telecast of The Four Divas on Fairfax Cable

Television. Ms. Crowder has sung a wide variety of operatic roles and she performed the original title role in the world premiere of Michael Ching's opera *Faith* with OperaFest of New Hampshire.

Toni has performed as a guest soloist with various orchestras including, Ra'anana Orchestra Tel Aviv, The Albany Symphony, The Mid-Atlantic Wind Symphony, The Lynchburg Symphony Orchestra, The Rappahannock Pops Orchestra, Old Bridge Chamber Orchestra, and The Georgetown University Chamber Orchestra. Ms. Crowder has sung in Italy with diverse performances at the Villa Contarini, Monselice, singing the role of Santuzza from *Cavalleria Rusticana*, as well as concerts at the Basicilica di S. Maria Assunta in Bango di Romagna and the Chiesa di San Martino in Este with internationally acclaimed tenor Maurizio Saltarin.

As an Artist-in-Residence, she has helped students from extremely diverse backgrounds create and produce original operas. Her residencies were sponsored through the Virginia Commission of the Arts and The National Endowment for the Arts. Ms. Crowder's residency work was recognized through the *Richmond Times Dispatch*, Richmond Channel Five News, and *The Free Lance Star*, Fredericksburg, VA. The Virginia Music Educators Association and the National Federation of Music Clubs featured her as a guest clinician to present about her residence experiences.

Denise and Toni are available for workshops, book readings, and seminars related to the mindfulness of singing. Email mindfulnessofsinging@gmail.com to discuss how they might serve your choir, book club or mindfulness community.

Printed in Poland
by Amazon Fulfillment
Poland Sp. z o.o., Wrocław